John Bleecker Miller

Trade Organizations in Politics

Or, Federalism in Cities

John Bleecker Miller

Trade Organizations in Politics
Or, Federalism in Cities

ISBN/EAN: 9783337132583

Printed in Europe, USA, Canada, Australia, Japan

Cover: Foto ©ninafisch / pixelio.de

More available books at **www.hansebooks.com**

Trade Organizations

in Politics

or

Federalism in Cities.

by

J. Bleecker Miller.

NEW YORK:
OXFORD PUBLISHING COMPANY.

1887.

Entered, according to Act of Congress, in the year 1887, by
J. BLEECKER MILLER,
in the Office of the Librarian of Congress, at Washington, D. C.

THE MCWILLIAMS PRINTING COMPANY,
81 and 83 Elm Street, New York.

TO

M. DUANE JONES,

THIS BOOK IS RESPECTFULLY DEDICATED.

CONTENTS.

	PAGE.
TRADE ORGANIZATIONS IN PUBLIC AFFAIRS,	1
FEDERALISM AND THE SOCIAL CONTRACT THEORY,	61
UNIVERSAL SUFFRAGE IN CITIES,	118
ARGUMENT ON THE ALDERMANIC BILL,	135
PROGRESS AND ROBBERY:	
I. A PROPERTY OWNER'S ANSWER,	153
II. A BUSINESS MAN'S ANSWER,	175
III. A WORKINGMAN'S ANSWER,	185
PROGRESS AND JUSTICE,	201

INTRODUCTION.

Considering the attention now given to the participation of trade organizations in public affairs, it occurred to me that the following papers, containing some thoughts on this subject, might be of general interest. The first essay, on "Trade Organizations in Public Affairs," was read before the Academy of Political Science in 1884, and treats of the subject from a historical point of view. The second, on "Federalism and the Social Contract Theory," was read before the German Gesellig-Wissenschaftlicher Verein, of this city, in 1883, and is a review of the opposing theories. The third paper, on "Universal Suffrage in Cities," is an argument in favor of the application of the theory advocated in the first essay to the election of our legislators, and was read before the Young Men's Democratic Club in 1885. The fourth is a speech in favor of the application of the same principle to the election of Aldermen, and was delivered at a hearing on the Aldermanic bill before Governor Hill in the same year. Of the next three papers, which were intended to counteract the false start of the trade organizations made last Fall, two are speeches delivered during that campaign against the heresies of Henry George, and the other was written since then on the same subject. The last article, entitled "Progress and Justice," is an attempt to show that the recent communistic campaign does not affect the correctness of the theories advocated by me in 1883, and that only by persistently following out those ideas on which our federal government was formed can a satisfactory solution of the great problems of the day be attained. I wish here to acknowledge my indebtedness to the writings of Stahl, Marlo, Von Mohl and the Professorial Socialists, Brentano, Schmoller, Gierke and others, although their books are written with but little reference to American affairs; and among American writers, I have obtained valuable suggestions from Walker, Gladden, Cherouny and Professor Adams of Cornell University.

The papers, with the exception of the second essay, have been left in their original form. They consequently contain some repetition, but this also makes each one to a certain extent complete in itself, which may not be disagreeable to readers in this busy city of New York. They are all attempts to develop the same idea, namely, that a city should be a political unit in its relations to the State, and that its inhabitants should be allowed to express their political convictions, unhampered by a division into geographical election districts, by which means the trade, business and professional organizations will gradually and peaceably come to take their due part in our public affairs, thereby striking at the root of our main political and economical evils. In my opinion, this change in our government is the one most needed, and must precede all successful attempts to permanently improve our civil service, our methods of transportation, our liquor license laws, our tenement house system, and all the most urgently demanded reforms of the day.

Trade Organizations in Public Affairs.

I.

SELF-GOVERNMENT AND REPRESENTATION OF GROUPS OF MEN WITH COMMON MATERIAL INTERESTS.

MEN, having certain wishes in common, naturally unite in groups in order to carry out those wishes, because they can by their united energy supply many of their wants more easily than by their individual efforts.

The strongest want among all men is for the means required for their physical existence; after these have been supplied, so far as absolutely necessary, and their protection from the attacks of others secured, they desire to satisfy other wishes, such as that to exercise their sympathy, to worship the deity, to develop their fancy, to increase their knowledge, etc.

With the object of better carrying out these various wishes, we see that men have united from the earliest times, in various groups, beginning with associations of hunters to capture large quantities of game, or to drive others from their hunting grounds; then uniting to exercise their sympathy by punishing some individual, for wronging another, who is too weak to retaliate; then meeting together to propitiate the deity and supporting a common intercessor or priest.

But with the beginning of agricultural life, the wants of man's physical body to be supplied by common efforts increase greatly; wells must be dug, land must be cleared and drained, heavy weights lifted. The necessity for a ready defence against outsiders and against evil-disposed neighbors increases; consequently, the union becomes closer and common action more frequent. To provide for these most important matters, some organization must be provided, with means at its disposal to meet sudden emergencies, and to provide so far as possible for future wants; these means must be contributed by the men who have possessions, and they naturally select the persons who shall have charge of these common matters, although frequent meetings are customary on important questions. Thus begins self-government. Thereby, gradually, the sympathy of members for each other increases, and help for the unfortunate and revenge for the injured becomes a more general practice. With a more regular mode of life, and less uncertainty for the future, grows the habit of looking ahead, and the benefits of superior knowledge and thought become more apparent; hence religion and common education receive more attention. Then neighboring groups of agriculturists find that they have wants in common; roads must be built, streams bridged, markets held for the mutually beneficial exchange of their commodities, and meetings to consider and provide for these common interests must be had through representatives, since all cannot conveniently attend.

The modern materialistic school would have us believe that it is only these physical necessities and dangers which are the mainsprings of human action; but men have also other wants.

Thus it becomes possible for groups of men with the same material interests, living some distance apart, to act in common for their furtherance and protection. The duties and rights of these representatives of common material interests of different neighborhoods increase with the number of common wants, caused by the progress of civilization, and with the danger from attacks by common foes. To provide for these, means must be furnished by well-to-do persons, in both communities, and permanent officials appointed to take charge of them. Thus representative government begins.

In time, sympathy spreads and increases, until misfortune or wrong suffered by men in neighboring villages leads to united action. Subsequently, by intercourse, especially with outsiders, the wits of the people are sharpened, and the advantages to be acquired by higher education and better religious services become apparent, and larger unions are formed for raising the necessary means to support their teachers and pastors, who are often induced to come from foreign lands.

The supervision of these other common wants is generally left to the same persons who were appointed primarily only to further the common material interests, since by the similar occupation, in the same geographical division, a similar mode of life and a similarity of ideas on most important subjects is formed, although, in exceptional cases, special unions are formed to gratify some other peculiarly strong desire, which intersects the various unions for material interests.

If men have, in common, desires arising from their common method of gaining a livelihood, their sense of self-preservation will not let them rest, until they have united to secure their fulfilment and preservation, and thus ever larger circles, or groups of groups, may be formed, each intended, however, to embrace a smaller number of vital interests.

Thus, one person generally belonged to two or more groups of individuals, each with certain common interests, whose sphere of action decreased as the number of its component members or groups increased. The progress and prosperity of mankind has consisted in the increase of the number of these groups, at the same rate that common interests increased, and in entrusting each with the duty of furthering the interests common to that group, and no others.

How urgent and numerous the interests of each group may be, and how numerous and powerful consequently must be the officials who watch over these interests, depends upon circumstances. A modern state is, or ought to be, such a group of groups of men, whose common material interests are so strong that they are willing to defend those interests in common, and whose sympathy is so strong that they are willing to submit their mutual differences to peaceful decision—arbitration.

But men are only too apt to depart from this ideal Germanic form of self and representative government, misled, especially, by theories derived from other, older, races; one group invades the province of another, and undertakes to fulfill its duties, or destroy its existence; men are slow to recognize the growth of new circles with common material interests, caused by a change in the manner of earning a livelihood, and cling to old associations or try to adopt their forms to satisfy new and different wants; men fail to see that by the improvement of the means of communication, etc., the existence of new and larger circles becomes possible, and continue instead to plod along in the individualistic struggle and thus lose the saving of energy which united action would cause. Or men, misled again by the examples of others, form unions containing a larger number of individuals, than actually have interests or sympathies, in common, or undertake to perform, in common, work which really belongs to smaller associations.

Among the principal wants which such a state, or a circle of men with common material interests, united with other circles for the furtherance of interests common to all, seek to satisfy are the following: They seek to have the share which each group must contribute to the common fund as small as possible, and collected in a manner as little burdensome as possible, *i.e.*, they have an interest in tax legislation. They strive to protect themselves from the unfair acts of some other group of the same state with whom they come most frequently in contact, and by which they suffer more than the members of any other group, *i.e.*, they have an interest in internal legislation and litigation. They endeavor to protect themselves against the unfair acts of men belonging to some other state, by which they suffer more than the other groups of their state; *i.e.*, they have an interest in the relations of the state with foreign governments. These wants, common wants of various circles, require that they should be represented in the government of the State.

The men belonging to the same circle have also an interest in satisfying all their common wants by united efforts; in stopping dishonest work, whereby the produce of all is brought into disrepute; in exercising the greater sympathy, which they in time get to feel for members of the same group, by revenging their injuries and allaying their sufferings. These wants require that each group should retain a certain amount of self-government.

Whenever men cannot satisfy their wants they are dissatisfied, and whenever groups of men have such unsatisfied wishes, the whole group is affected by this dissatisfaction. One group of men often asserts and enforces its wishes over other groups, and undertakes or pretends to undertake, to interpret and fulfill the wishes of the members of these groups; but men, with the best intentions, cannot understand other people's wishes so well as they do themselves, nor fulfill them as exactly. If this attempt is persevered in too long and too recklessly, the groups whose wishes are disregarded will at last undertake to assert them, without recourse to regular means provided by government; men begin to object to supporting the old means provided by law for the alleged realizing of these wants; complaints of their expense and their insufficiency become frequent, and if these do not receive attention, and the wishes of the new groups are not supplied, revolution follows.

The wishes which groups of men gaining a livelihood by the same means have in common, exceed in intensity and number those which the people as a whole have in common, *i. e.*, the so-called natural or original rights of life, limb, etc. When one group has usurped an undue amount of authority over another group, the appeal to these original rights is made, in order to get rid of these oppressions by the oppressed group, but so soon as these wrongs are remedied and the group is allowed to regulate its own affairs, it begins anew the construction of regulations for itself contrary to or supplementary of the system of so-called original rights, under whose banner they have just been fighting.

No populous nation with different material interests is ever content to live together, under legislation concerning only the few general interests common to all; **man's self-interest is too strong.**

II.

THE GERMANIC TOWN: AN ASSOCIATION OF FARMERS WITH COMMON INTERESTS.

WE are all familiar with the **Germanic** group of men, seeking a livelihood by agriculture in a given neighborhood, under the same conditions of soil and climate, and united with other similar communities, in more or less intimate unions, according to the extent of their common interests, and yielding to the common will of the unions in all matters affecting those common interests, and exercising themselves all other power over themselves; we call this the township system, with its principle of self-government and representation.

As to the admirable working of this system, all are agreed: The common interests are understood and ably defended in the body of representatives, against those of other towns or groups of towns; justice is administered by neighbors in a fair, considerate manner; the poor are provided for, although a proper pride urges them not to become a burden on their neighbors; the bad cultivation of the ground is condemned by public opinion and sometimes by local ordinances.

Nowhere has the natural formation of Germanic agricultural communities been more favored by circumstances than in New England; in fact, it seems as though at that time no model existed for them in Europe. In England, the Anglo-Saxon "tuns" had become manors, as is shown in Seebohm's recent work on the "English Village Community;" if anywhere, it must have been in the old Frisian "mark," in the north of Holland, that the Puritans found the prototypes for their communities.

No better description of a model Germanic association, enjoying the full right of self-government and representation has been given than that of the New England township, by De Tocqueville in his "Democracy in America:" "Its average population is from two to three thousand; so that, on the one hand, the interests of the inhabitants are not likely to conflict, and, on the other, men capable of conducting its affairs are always to be found among its citizens" (page 63).

"The New Englander is attached to his township . . . because it constitutes a strong and free social body of which he is a member, and whose government claims and deserves the exercise of his sagacity" (page 68). "The township and the county are therefore bound to take care of their special interests" (page 83).

I will only further cite the description in Palfrey's "History of New England," Vol. Ii., p. 12: "To the utmost extent consistent with the common action and the common welfare of the aggregate of towns that make the State, the towns severally are empowered to take care of those interests of theirs which they respectively can best understand, and can most efficiently and most economically provide for; and these are identical with the interests which most directly concern the public security, comfort and morals."

That these beauties of the township government are still acknowledged is shown by Governor Seymour's article, on the "Government of the United States," in the "North American Review," of 1878, p. 367: "Upon such questions, so far as they particularly concern them, the people of the towns are more intelligent and more interested than those outside of their limits can be. The theory of self-government is not founded upon the idea that the people are necessarily virtuous and intelligent, but it attempts to distribute each particular power to those who have the greatest interest in its wise and faithful exercise."

But these New England towns were not mere aggregates of a certain number of individuals—as was proper in an agricultural community; the town meetings were attended only by freeholders or by men with some interest in land, within the township. Thus Palfrey in his second volume, page 14, says: "The land, when its bounds had been set out by a Committee of the Court, was held at first by the company as proprietors in common. To transact the joint business . . . . the organization of a local authority was immediately needed."

This was thoroughly in accord with the system of the old Germanic "mark," in which rights and duties might be said to be attached to the lots of land, and exercised only by the owners of the land. (Gierke, Vol. II., p. 92). The mark and town were both associations of agriculturists, united to further their common interests.

III.

SELF-GOVERNMENT AND REPRESENTATION OF FARMERS, WITH COMMON INTERESTS SECURED BY THE CONSTITUTION.

THIS necessity for representation and self-government for groups of men with similar material interests was thoroughly understood and appreciated by the Fathers who formed our Constitution. The Revolution had been brought about by one group of men attempting to deny the right of the expression of their wishes by other groups of men, engaged in seeking a livelihood by common means, as to the manner and extent of their contributions toward the expenses of attaining certain ends, which the latter had greatly desired. "Taxation without representation is tyranny," was the cry, and when that danger to their common material interests had united and roused the men of America to arms, and nerved them through a seven years' war, the Fathers took good care that this principle should be recognized in our government.

The speeches on the adoption of the Constitution in the different States are full of declarations that men united according to their means of gaining a livelihood, *i. e.*, according to their interests, should be represented in government, and that this new government should be restricted to those common interests; these principles were nowhere denied; this is shown by the following three citations, whose number might be greatly increased:

In the New York Convention, on June 23, 1778, Chancellor Livingston said: "As to the idea of representing the feelings of the people, I do not entirely understand it, unless by their feelings are meant their *interests*. They appear to me to be the same thing. But, if they have feelings which do not rise out of their interests, I think they ought not to be represented." (Elliot, II., p. 275.)

In the Virginia Convention, Mr. Corbin said: "What is the criterion of representation? Do the people wish land only to be represented? They have their wish; for the qualifications which the laws of the States require to entitle a man to vote for a State representative, are the qualifications required by this plan to vote for a representative to Congress; and in this State, and in most of the others, the possession of a freehold is necessary to entitle a man to the privilege of a vote. (Elliot, III., p. 110.)

Mr. Nicholas spoke to the same effect: "We find there is a decided majority [of electors] attached to the landed interest; consequently, the landed interest must prevail in the choice. Should the State be divided into districts, in no one can the mercantile interest by any means have an equal weight in the elections; therefore, the former will be more fully represented in Congress.", (Elliot, III., p. 9.)

The *Federalist* also fully recognizes the necessity of representing the *various* interests of the citizens, as is shown, for example, by the two following extracts:

Letter No. 55: "Taking each State by itself its laws are the same, and its interests but little diversified. A few men, therefore, will possess all the knowledge requisite for a proper representation of them. Were the interests and affairs of each individual State perfectly simple and uniform, a knowledge of them in one part would involve a knowledge of them in every other, and the whole State might be completely represented by a single member taken from any part of it. . . . At present, some of the States are little more than a society of husbandmen. Few of them have made much progress in those branches of industry which give a variety and complexity to the affairs of a nation. . . . A representative for every 30,000 inhabitants will render the latter both a safe and a competent guardian of the interests which will be confided to it."

Letter No. 58: "A landed interest, a manufacturing interest, a mercantile interest, a moneyed interest, with many lesser interests, grow up of necessity in civilized nations. . . . The regulation of these various and interfering interests forms the principal task of modern legislation."

There is nothing surprising in the fact that the agricultural interest was uppermost in the minds of the founders of the Republic, and generally referred to, to the exclusion of other interests. For the census returns show that in 1790 only three per cent. of the population lived in cities with more than 8,000 inhabitants.

The first constitutions of almost all the States required, as stated in the extract of the speech of Mr. Corbin above quoted, an interest in real estate as a qualification for voters. The first constitution of any size, the Bill of Rights, of 1776, of Virginia—the State of Henry and Jefferson—says in §6: "All men having sufficient evidence of permanent common interest with, and attachment to the community, have the right of suffrage;" and in that State the property qualification was not removed until 1850.

The Massachusetts constitution of 1780 allowed only male inhabitants, who were freeholders, to vote; that of South Carolina, adopted 1790, required ownership of freehold; that of Georgia, of 1777, required of the voter a possession of £10, or to belong to a mechanic trade. The constitution of New York, of 1777, which served generally as the model for subsequent constitutions, and which might be called the first of constitutions, as distinguished from the previous Bills of Rights, or Declarations of General Principles, required that voters for the Assembly must have freeholds of £20, or have rented a tenement in the county of the yearly value of 40 shillings; but for Senators only freeholders possessed of franchise of over £100 might vote. The fact that this system had brought to the front the noblest men the world has ever seen, justified their appreciation of it. This property qualification was not entirely removed till 1846. Representatives were, moreover, required to be landowners, long after the necessity of that qualification was removed for voters.

Thus, Madison could say: "If those ten men, who were to be chosen, be elected by landed men, and have land themselves, can the electors have anything to apprehend?" (Elliot, III., p. 332.) And Governor Randolph: "The representatives are chosen by and from among the people. They will have a fellow-feeling for the farmers and planters. . . . What laws can they make that will not operate on themselves and friends, as well as on the rest of the people?" (Elliot, III., pp. 470 and 120.)

While these extracts show how highly the right of representation was valued by these agricultural communities, and how the necessity for the representation of their most vital interests was understood, the self-government in all matters which did not concern all the people was most jealously guarded. Many of the speakers in the Constitutional Conventions denied that any such common interest existed; this almost led to the rejection of the United States Constitution. Luther Martin, in his very elaborate and powerful speech before the Legislature of Maryland, in 1787, declared: "We considered the system proposed (the United States Constitution) to be the most complete, most abject system of slavery that the wit of man ever devised under the pretense of forming a government for free states." In fact, the Constitution would very possibly not have been adopted, if it had not been generally understood that the amendment, declaring that all rights not expressly granted were reserved to the people and the States, would be adopted.

While this dread of centralization in the national government was thus shown, no less opposition doubtless existed to the idea that the State governments had absolute sovereignty, in the sense in which that word is used by Austin and many modern writers.

The State governments had been formed in the midst of troublesome times after the model of the colonial governments; these certainly possessed no unlimited powers, and no intention to make a radical new departure can be shown. The members of the legislature were not chosen, as at present, by divisions of counties, but were elected by the county on what we would call a general ticket—so that they represented not a mere number of individuals, but the counties or groups of associated individuals.

Not till 1846 were the supervisors authorized, in this State, to divide counties into election districts.

This autonomy of these associations, smaller than the State, is most clearly seen in the New England States, where that Germanic institution had had fullest opportunity to develop itself. Thus, De Tocqueville says in his above cited "Democracy in America," on pages 67 and 66: "It is important to remember that they [the towns] have not been invested with privileges, but that they seem, on the contrary, to have surrendered a portion of their independence to the State. . . . I believe that not a man is to be found who would acknowledge that the State had any right to interfere in their local interests. . . . Hence arises the maxim that every one is the best and sole judge of his own private interest. . . . The township taken as a whole, and in relation to the government of the country, may be looked upon as an individual to whom the theory I have just alluded to is applied."

The statutes of Connecticut (Title 7, ch. 2 of Revision of 1874) recognize this reserved right in the people of the towns to make such regulations for their welfare, not concerning matters of a criminal nature, nor repugnant to the laws of the State, as they deem expedient.

In fact the town, county, state and national government were all of at least equal importance, and to no one of them were the people supposed to have surrendered absolute authority. The sovereignty, if that is a proper term, remained in the people, which could intrust portions of it at different times to the government of these larger or smaller associations, as the common interests of that association demanded. In the words of Elbridge Gerry: "We are neither the same nation, nor different nations. We ought not, therefore, to pursue the one or the other of these ideas too closely." If anywhere, it was in the smallest association that the greatest power resided.

In the words of Governor Seymour, in the article in the "North American Review," above cited: "When we have secured good government in towns and counties, most of the objects of government are gained. In the ascending scale of rank, in the descending scale of importance is the legislature."

We see, therefore, that the men of the Revolution did not regard the inhabitants of this country as a mere number of individuals, but as associations of men seeking a common livelihood, whose interests as members of these associations, required to be represented in the government; and that the great fear at that time was, that the numerically larger association would interfere with the rights and duties of the smaller associations.

The fact that the people consisted almost entirely of "husbandmen" made the geographical divsion of election districts the only proper one; only thus could they be enabled to send representatives of their real interests to the legislatures; with what opposition would a proposition have been met, that 15,000 inhabitants of tobacco-growing Virginia should vote for one representative, together with 15,000 farmers of New Hampshire! They could not foresee that within so short a time—by the application of steam and the progress of science—so many new means of extracting force, *i. e.*, obtaining the means of livelihood from other substances than the earth, would be discovered; and that thereby men would be freed from the necessity of direct connection with the soil, and could thus support themselves in large numbers, in a small space, by manipulating the detached products of the soil.

IV.

GROWTH OF CITIES AND OF MEANS OF OBTAINING A LIVING OTHER THAN BY FARMING.

ACCORDING to the census of 1790, three and one-third per cent. of our total population lived in cities with more than 8,000 inhabitants; according to the last census over 50 per cent. of the people of the State of New York lived in such cities.

The positive and relative growth of city life is shown by the following table of the population of the State and of the City of New York, in the ten census reports:

	1790.	1800.	1810.	1820.
The population of New York State.	340,120	589,051	959,049	1,372,111
The population of New York City..	33,131	60,515	93,373	123,706
	1830.	1840.	1850.	1860.
The population of New York State.	1,918,608	2,428,921	3,097,394	3,880,735
The population of New York City..	202,589	312,710	515,547	813,669
	1870.	1880.		
The population of New York State.	4,382,759	5,082,871		
The population of New York City..	942,292	1,206,299		

We see, therefore, that the ratio of the population of the city to the State has increased from less than one-tenth to nearly one-quarter, and that the city has now four times as many inhabitants as the State had in 1790. The United States now have an urban population of 13,000,000, and New York State has 58 cities of over 8,000 inhabitants, with a total urban population of 2,726,367.

Well may this age be called the era of great cities, and to no State does this apply better than to our own.

V.

ABOLITION OF REAL ESTATE QUALIFICATION FOR VOTERS.

THE only change in our political system, to correspond to this total change in our daily life and business occupation, has been to abolish the qualification of ownership of real estate for the exercise of the franchise, under the influence of the theories of the Democratic party.

One of the chief causes of the fall of the Federal party was its failure to recognize and provide for this change of the population; as Hamilton said in his plan for "The Christian Constitutional Society :" "The populous cities ought particularly to be attended to.... The cities have been employed by the Jacobins to give an impulse to the country." But his plan was not carried out—even if it could have been successful, and the discontent of the inhabitants of cities was not removed.

This change was accomplished in this State substantially by the Constitutional Convention of 1821. The debates show that it was a contest between the desire of the growing population of cities for political power to protect their interests, and the wish of the agricultural communities to preserve their preponderance.

Chancellor Kent said : " It is to protect this important class of the community [farmers], that the Senate should be preserved. It should be the representative of the landed interest. . . . It 1773, New York City contained only 21,000 inhabitants, in 1821 123,000 souls ! . . and it is no hazardous prophecy to foretell that in less than a century, that city will govern the State. And can gentlemen seriously and honestly say, that no danger is to be apprehended from those combustible materials which such a city must ever enclose?" (page 116 of Clarke's Constitutional Debates). And Judge Spencer argued: "The landed interest of this State must thus be at the mercy of a description of men who have no solid and permanent interest in your institutions" (page 115 ib.).

In favor of the abolition of the property qualification, Mr. Buel claimed: "The city population will never be able to depress that of the country. . . . From what combination of other interests can danger arise to the landed interests? The mercantile and manufacturing interests are the only ones which can obtain a formidable influence" (p. 124 ib.).

Mr. Van Buren, in a very able and elaborate speech, showed that New York City paid taxes on sixty-nine millions dollars worth of property, being twenty-seven millions more than the eastern district, and twenty-four millions more than the middle district, and fourteen millions more than the western district; and yet the western district sends nine senators, the middle district nine, the eastern eight, and New York City one senator.

This claim of the inhabitants of cities to have their interests represented was granted, in principle, by abolishing the requirement of land ownership for the franchise; but, unfortunately, the reform stopped there, and no plan for representing the various real interests of the inhabitants of cities was devised. Perhaps the chief reason herefor was the prevalence, at that time, of the theories of Rousseau, transplanted by Jefferson, which made the only object of government the assertion of the so-called rights of men, and recognized the need of no associations for a people, except one almighty state, as described in my last year's lecture on the history of the social contract theory. This theory was very useful here, as in France, for tearing down antiquated institutions, but it also prevented the adoption of the new forms of government and representation, necessary for the new groupings of men with common material interests in cities.

Thus, the strongest champion of the citizens in the Convention of 1821, Mr. Root, had declared: "We have no different estates having different interests, necessary to be guarded from encroachment by the watchful eye of jealousy. We are all the same estate—all commoners. . . . These powerful checks may be necessary between different families possessing adverse interests, but can never be salutary among brothers of the same family, whose interests are similar."

In compliance with this Utopian theory, the inhabitants of cities were admitted to the franchise, divided for convenience of voting into artificial groups of men, living near a certain polling booth.

This was not even the theory of Rousseau, for his school contemplated the existence of small agricultural communities, in which all citizens could meet at once in a public meeting; the great cities of even his day and the large countries of Europe were deemed misfortunes to be remedied. In fact, our present city governments are an accidental growth, formed by attempting to copy too closely theories and practices, which work well in agricultural communities, where alone men are divided into groups having common material interests, by geographical lines.

VI.

UNSCIENTIFIC CHARACTER OF OUR THEORY OF CITY GOVERNMENT.

NO writers on political science justify our city governments. In the writings of the Fathers, few, if any, references are found to city government; more modern writers on political science shake their heads and pass by on the other side, to the more attractive subject of township government, as if the form of government for thirteen millions of our most industrious and wealthy citizens did not deserve as much attention as the hackneyed subject of the New England town. Lieber states: "Though I own that one of the problems we have yet to solve is how to unite in large cities the highest degree of individual liberty and order" (p. 392).

Woolsey, in his "Political Economy," acknowledges that "a township where there is a scattered population with at most a village or two, needs one kind of government, while a city with a compact population needs another," (p. 366), and "that for some reason or other our present system [of city government] is exceedingly bad, the experience of New York will prove," (p. 369), but as to a remedy he confines himself to a few antiquated suggestions concerning the introduction of a property qualification.

Governor Seymour, in his article entitled "The Government of the United States," in the *North American Review* of 1878, in which he lauds the local township government, as the political unit of our nation, to which our greatness is due, has nothing to say for us inhabitants of cities, except : " Its [the township government] workings are more clearly seen in the country than in cities."

Of foreign writers, I will only cite Professor Gneist in his article on the " Government of the City of London " (p. 52 in Von Holtzendorf's " Popular Writings "): "Among all communities, the cities in their unexpected, gigantic growth are still unsolved problems for the legislator ; " and "a city in which a party wall makes inhabitants greater strangers than miles of distance, can not be organized on the simple plan of a peasant community or a stock company."

And as President Woolsey states, on p. 384 of his work, above cited : "A general law for town administration is easier to be framed than for cities with varying and vast interests " (p. 384).

No one knows better than the citizens of New York how far these words fall short of describing the actual condition of our government. The " vast and varying interests " of the inhabitants of this city are represented in the Board of Aldermen almost exclusively by liquor dealers, whose regular characteristic joke is to hang their overcoats and plug hats on two busts of American statesmen—and who have not yet organized this year, owing to the desire of a fraction of the majority to make a liquor dealer whose appearance would make him a marked man in any assembly of merchants, tradesmen, or master mechanics, president. The cry to deprive the Board of Aldermen of every power, and even to abolish it, is becoming stronger : it is recognized as an anachronism. The Board has now been reduced to a state of helplessness, incompatible with the needs of our growing city ; for example, it cannot raise money even to employ a stenographer to make an investigation. Many of the departments are entirely independent, and all real power over the finances has been assumed by the mysterious

Board of Estimate and Apportionment, which determines the appropriation for each department, once for all, before the beginning of the year—a plan necessarily inconvenient and extravagant—but which all prefer to trusting our "representatives" with the city finances. In the Legislature our "varying and vast interests" are represented also to a large extent by liquor dealers, although there are several well-meaning, respectable lawyers in the delegation. One of these is chairman of the Committee on Commerce, and, as he acknowledged after his appointment, he knew the difference between a canal-boat and a Cunarder; but that was all he knew about commerce. In Congress, the delegation is smaller and more respectable, in proportion but no one claims that it fairly represents our "varying and vast interests." the legal profession predominates, to the exclusion of other trades and professions, as much in Congress as the liquor dealers do in the Board of Aldermen. more than half of the present Congress are lawyers.

As to self-government in cities, there is even less of that than of representation. The nearest approach to it for the 1,200,000 citizens, is the party caucus in the election district; if a man happens to hear where it is to be held, and if he attends, the browbeating and contempt with which unknown faces are treated prevent a second attempt. The District and Police Courts have in certain cases a jurisdiction limited to their district, that is about all the self-government there is in this city. The election districts are mapped out in a curious manner, with the professed attempt to bring an equal number of voters in each but in fact the object of laying out the districts was generally to secure to some little political boss the assured control of his "deestrick" by an appropriate arrangement of his friends and foes. The average citizen does not know the limit of his district; he has but the slightest interests in common with the unknown men with whom he is called on to elect a "representative," or the only local magistrate, the District Court Judge.

And yet the inhabitants of cities are not different beings from the farmers; like them, they are groups of men whose most important interest is to gain an honest, steady living; like them, they want to keep their business or trade from being injured by men with other and opposing interests; like them, they want to exercise a certain control over dishonest fellow professional or tradesmen, who are injuring their business by dishonest work.

In short, you may apply every description of a township to a trade, business or professional organization of men living in cities; but to apply that description to one of our geographical election districts is the bitterest irony.

VII.

HISTORICAL ORIGIN OF OUR THEORY OF CITY GOVERNMENT.

HOW has it come, then, that the government of all modern cities is based upon this plan of dividing a city by geographical lines? The answer is, that it is due, in the first place, in Europe, to the jealousy of royalty, supported by a land-owning nobility, of the power of citizens, united, according to the natural plan, *i. e.*, according to their interests. In England, for example, the tyrant Tudors began and the Stuarts finished the disorganization of the citizens, because they feared their opposition to absolute government.

The English cities existed long before charters were granted to them and, like those of the Continent, owe their growth and prosperity to the guild-associations of citizens according to their different trades, which in great part took the place of the older wards or frith-guilds, which consisted generally of land owners. The latter might be compared as to their origin to our Western Vigilance Committees. The following citations show how the old rural division into wards was replaced by the guilds of merchants, which term became synonymous with the city corporation; thus Glanville says that, if a villain have remained a year and a day in the city, "*ita quod in* COMMUNIAN, *scilicet* GYLDAM *tamquam civis receptus fuerit, eo ipso a villenagio liberabitur.*" (De Legibus, *lib.* v., c. 5.)

Brady's conclusion, in his English Burghs, published in 1700, is: "A free burgess was no other than a man that exercised free trade, according to the liberties and privileges of his burgh, whether he resided in it, or whether he had liberty to live and trade otherwhere " (p. 47).

The first city charters appear to have been granted in King John's time; that of Andever is granted "*hominibus de Andever quod habeant Gyldam Mercatoriam in Andever.*"

Norfolk had, in the twelfth year of Henry III., for its burgesses, merchants and traders at sea and upon the water.

In the time of Edward III., the whole government of the City of London was, for seventy years, in the hands of certain guilds; after that, a part of the power was given back to the wards, but the guilds still retain certain powers to this day.

The contest between land owners and traders in English cities was, however, never so violent as on the Continent, owing to the stronger central power of the English kings, but Toulmin Smith's Collection of the Charters of English Guilds shows to what a large extent these associations of tradesmen participated in the local and general affairs of government.

It was Henry VIII., and after him Edward VI., who by the confiscation of the property of the guilds and by their suppression, struck at the root of the liberties of English cities. Queen Elizabeth imposed heavy taxes on them, and the Stuarts naturally followed a similar policy.

The overthrow of real city government dates from the Restoration, when the old borroughs were called on to produce grants from the crown, as authority for their municipal rights. Jeffries denied that of London, with its oldest exclusive jurisdiction in the land; and the smaller burghs, intimidated by the treatment of London, made haste to surrender their old charters to the crown, and to receive in return new charters, in giving which good care was taken that all remains of municipal self-government, and the means of allowing citizens to unite according to their interests, were removed.

The government of cities was placed in the hands of artificial, small, select bodies, which could be easily managed by the crown, with whose selection or control the citizens had little or nothing to do. This legacy of the Stuart despotism was confirmed by William III., who was probably as little a friend of popular government as his predecessors; he confirmed the new charters, and in the words of Lieber: "Cities in England were considered in the last century chiefly with reference to parliamentary elections;" and since *that time* no thorough scientific study or treatment of the subject appears to have occupied the minds of England's great thinkers, although the cities have been confessedly hot-beds of crime and misery; changes have been made without system; and to-day, while a great clamor exists for the removal of the remains of these deformed remnants of guild-governments, no satisfactory substitute is suggested, except a general extension of the suffrage, which will give England the same experience which we have had since 1826. In the words of Professor Jameson: "It is not possible to set forth a single definite scheme of town-government and say, 'This was, in this reign, the form of municipal government in England."

Our earliest American charters date unfortunately from the age of Stuart despotism; that of New York was made probably under the personal supervision of James II., and under the illiberal George II, the charter was reaffirmed with additions, his attorney-general Bradley certifying that it contained nothing "prejudicial to the interests of his Majesty." Albany, the only other New York city, prior to the Revolution, received a similar so-called Dongan Charter.

The Mayor was to be appointed, the ordinances of the Board of Aldermen were to have force only for three months, etc. Of course, no provision is made for the organization of citizens according to their trades, etc., to protect their interests; James was not going to have in future, in American cities, the same organizations which had opposed the aspiration of his family in England; the citizens were to vote like countrymen, in wards where they resided. The contrast between this Stuart charter, with its mass of unorganized citizens, and the true Germanic city, is seen for example by a glance at the "Platform of Government" made by the New England Company, which had been chartered by James I. to settle New England, and which planted, in the Queen Ann Colony, the germ of New England government. This "platform" was dedicated, in 1662, to Prince Charles (afterwards Charles I.) and states "And there is no less care to be taken for the trade and public commerce of *merchants, whose government ought to be within themselves*, in respect of the several occasions arising between them"; and in another place, it states, that the merchants and mechanics should govern the cities.

How different might the history of American cities have been, had this colonization of the company not failed, and had it not been forced to give up its charter in 1635.

The colonization of New England proceeded then by Englishman, mostly from the agricultural districts of Eastern England. They formed good rural governments, but they saw no necessity for making any distinction for cities.

Thus, Palfrey in History of New England (vol. II., p. 12), declares: "In law a city is a town." And Dillon, on Municipal Corporations (p. 463), says: "In New England towns gradually merged into cities, and that which was done by the direct meeting of the citizens, is subsequently *attempted* to be accomplished by representatives." Before the Revolution, there were no chartered cities in New England. Boston was governed by select men until 1822.

From these two types, the one taken from the New England country town, and the other from the Stuart city, an endless number of variations have been formed which it is unnecessary here to follow; suffice it to say that none of them are satisfactory. It reminds one of De Tocqueville's description of France, under the Old Regime, before the revolution: "Civic rights were constantly bestowed, taken away, restored, increased, modified in thousand ways and unceasingly. No better indication of the contempt into which all local liberties had fallen can be found, than such eternal changes of the law which no one seemed to notice" (p, 371).

No wonder that our citizens have also lost all hope from so-called "tinkering with the charter," and have suffered a principle to become law, that, as Mr. Stern says, in the above quoted article: "The American city has no chartered privileges which anybody is bound to respect." See also: Kent's Commentaries, p. 275: "Such powers [of counties, cities, towns and villages] are subject to the control of the Legislature of the State." And in Darlington *vs.* Mayor of New York (31 N. Y., 164) Denio, J., held: "City Corporations are emanations of the supreme law-making power of the State." The principle that our Legislature possesses this power, claimed by the Stuarts, in this land of liberty, and against which, in other days, men have been so ready to stake their lives, and which makes all attempts at improvement, which at best can be but gradual, liable at any moment to be overthrown, has also been repeatedly affirmed by the United States Courts; for example, in United States *vs.* Railroad Company (17 Wall, 329) and New Orleans *vs.* Clark '95 United States, 653). Our State Courts have gove even further and declared that not only the city's public rights, but also the property owned by the city, as a corporation, is under the absolute control of the State, in People *vs.* Kerr in New York Court of Appeals (27 N. Y., 188).

As Mr. Stern says, in his article on cities, in "Lalor's Encyclopædia": "We have lost, in fact, though not in name, our chartered privileges as binding contracts with the State."

VIII.

OUR ROMAN LAW THEORY OF THE RELATION OF STATE AND CITY GOVERNMENT.

BESIDES the example of these cities, with charters designed by the Stuarts, a mistaken theory as to the origin of corporations in general, and their relation to the State, has tended to keep our municipalities in abject submission to the State.

The definition commonly placed at the beginning of treatises on corporations, is that of Chief Justice Marshall, in the Dartmouth College Case, that a corporation is "an artificial being, invisible, intangible, and existing *only in contemplation of law;*" and then follows Chancellor Kent's statement: "Public corporations are such as are created by the government for political purposes, as counties, cities, towns and villages." (Comm., II., p. 275.)

Since then public corporations are originated by the State, and exist "only in contemplation of law," it must follow that the State can change or abolish them at any time.

But is it an historical fact that the State formed all smaller unions for political purposes, such as counties, cities, towns, etc.?

Were not the Anglo-Saxon monarchies formed by a union of the inhabitants of various districts, which still exist as parishes? Was not the Heptarchy formed from a union of these monarchies, which continued later to exist, with more or less independence, as subdivisions of the kingdom of England? The shires and parishes and cities of England were not all created by the State; on the contrary, many of them existed before the State, and assisted in creating the State.

As Coke says, in 5 Reports, p. 64: "The inhabitants of a town without any custom, may make ordinances or by-laws for any such thing which is for the general good of the public, unless it is indeed pretended by any such by-law to abridge the general liberty of the people."

As to private associations, with the right to contract and hold property as an association, it is equally true that a formal incorporation was not originally required therefor.

Thus Kyd, in his work on Corporations (1793), says: "The capacity of contracting in a collective capacity, was not in ancient times [under Henry III.] confined to a corporation." The right of unincorporated associations to hold property is further shown by the statutes of Queen Elizabeth's time. (5th Eliz., c. 27.)

If we look on the continent of Europe, we see numberless associations, with all the rights now claimed by corporations, springing into existence without an act of the State, or, in many cases, where no State (according to the modern fashionable definition of the word) could be said to exist; we see them also uniting and forming themselves into modern States.

In fact, according to Germanic principles, the State did not create the corporations, but the corporations created the State.

In the Roman law it was different; there, especially the later Byzantine emperors, in their dread of any approach to popular freedom, made the sanction of the State an essential part of a corporation. This theory was particularly pleasing to the European monarchs, who wished to emulate the absolute power of the Roman monarch, and to hide their breach of Germanic customs under the mysterious cloak of the Pandects. Hence this theory was introduced in the time of the Tudors and Stuarts, and corporations were said to exist only by privilege granted by the sovereign.

Recollections of the old Germanic system still remained. Thus Coke says, (in I. Inst., 3*a*, Cities): "The parishioners, or inhabitants, or *probi homines of Dale*, or church-wardens, are not capable to purchase lands, but goods they are, *unless it were in ancient time when such grants were allowed.*"

And Dugdale, in his Warwickshire (1730), says: "They [guilds] were in use long before any formal licenses were granted them." (Page 188.)

And Kyd, in his above cited works, after mentioning the present rule, that an unincorporated association cannot hold land, says: "It is difficult to account for the establishment of this rule. . . . The Societies of the Inns of Court are not corporations; yet, in their collective capacities, they have held the property of the ground on which the chambers are built, ever since they were established."

The rule cannot be accounted for, however, like many other anomalies of our law, when we remember that it has been taken from the Roman law, and replaced an old Germanic rule which held the contrary.

So long as we neglect the study of the history of our Germanic institutions, we will continue to believe in such statements as that of Blackstone, on this subject (I., ch. 18): "The honor of originally inventing these political constitutions [corporations] entirely belongs to the Romans." This opinion is adopted by Chancellor Kent (vol. II., p. 269), and his words have been copied by subsequent writers almost verbatim; for example, in Angell and Ames, on Corporations, p. 37.

We see, therefore, that, according to the Germanic

theory, neither public nor private corporations are entirely dependent beings created by a higher power, subject to be changed at the whim of that almighty sovereignty; but that each association has its own sphere of legitimate action, within which the existence of the smallest is entitled to as much respect as the largest, and that all come from the same source, *i. e.*, the people.

IX.

INSUFFICIENCY OF PROPOSED REMEDIES FOR OUR CITY GOVERNMENT.

WE see, therefore, that our present plan of division of inhabitants of cities fails to secure them real self-government or representation of their interests in the legislative bodies; that this plan is not sustained by authority of political authors; that its origin entitles it to no veneration or respect; that its practical workings are unsatisfactory.

The evils of our New York city government are only a little greater than those of Philadelphia, Boston, etc.; the description of an election in London, given by Prof. Gneist, in the article above cited, bears a strong resemblance to one of our own.

But yet it will not do to sit passively and say that "God made the country, but man made the city," or to consider our great cities, as Bismarck did, as excrescences on the body politic; for, in another century, our cities will probably exceed in size those of to-day, as much as the latter do those of the Revolution.

And yet, according to Mr. Stern's above quoted article in the "North American Review," the indebtedness of our eighteen largest cities (excluding New Orleans), from 1860 to 1875, has increased 270.9 per cent., and the taxation has increased 362.2 per cent., and the population 70.5 per cent. The States with the largest urban populations are Pennsylvania and New York, and are these not the States in which legislative scandals are most numerous?

Does this not prove that there is some radical defect in our system of self-government and of representation in cities?

The only important remedy which has been suggested is that the franchise should be restricted by a property qualification; a few gentlemen proposed such a measure in the Constitutional Convention of 1867—1868, and more recently, but the intense popular odium which this proposition attached to all who were connected with it, probably removes this plan from the field of practical politics. But the plan is also theoretically indefensible; it would unite the owners of property, according to its value, but it would not unite men according to their many other real interests, and would shut out a large number of people who have important, permanent interests in the proper government of the community; it would be the natural result of the heartless materialistic philosophy of the day. It would introduce into the New World cities the fierce contests which distracted European cities in the Middle Ages, between real-estate owners and the associations of tradesmen, and would end probably, as in former times, with the victory of the latter. If elections were held on a general ticket, and the power of the Mayor increased, this would perhaps somewhat improve matters, by removing the evils in the present system of pseudo self-government and representation in our geographical election districts; but no one will consider a plan satisfactory which would leave over a million people—more than one-third of the population of this country when the Constitution was formed—without a voice to represent its various interests, and which would hand over the immense power, necessary to govern such an unorganized mass, to one man, and would leave the people only the power of selecting that man, at stated intervals.

That was the ideal state of Napoleon III.; "the plebiscite is the republic," and it is merely an acknowlegment that self-government is a failure, and that we prefer an open, responsible boss to one who works through the forms of an unsuitable government although he may preserve the appearance of popular power. This is generally the cause of the growth of despotism.

The fact is that in our great cities, with their unorganized masses of voters, a political oligarchy has grown up, whose common interest it is to preserve the present helplessness of well-meaning citizens, by allowing them to unite only in an artificial group, according to geographical lines, which the popular voice has rightly dubbed "the machine," *i. e.*, an instrument, which has no life in itself, but is run by power from outside, to suit others' purposes. It is in order to preserve this system that the "honored leaders" ring the changes on "individualism," so that the people may not hear the forging of their chains in these very "Halls," which, by their strict centralization of power, give the lie direct to their professions. By the same cry, before the War, the poor white-trash in the South was humbugged by the slave-holding obligarchy. The great corporations with their consolidated power have also an interest in preserving this powerless individualism. Chauncey M. Depew spoke not without a purpose at the dinner on Evacuation Day, substantially as follows: "The great principle, declared when the British flag was torn down, was the liberty of the individual and his right and ability to govern himself."

General organizations of well-meaning citizens with committees of nine, twenty-four, fifty, seventy, one hundred, etc., have been tried again and again, and found wanting; Irving Hall, the Young Men's Democratic Club, the County Democracy, the Citizens' Committee were started by some of the best and shrewdest men in the city, but they all went the same road. The New Democracy, which in these days Mr. Roosevelt is trying to organize, can have no other future; he states that the plan of the County Democracy was good, but that the "bosses" got hold of it—and so they will of any artificial, machine organization of men, in geographical election districts; even the Republican papers acknowledge this morning that the new Republican organizations are practically in the hands of the old bosses.* The law for the protection of honest voting at primaries will only cause protoprimaries to be held, in which candidates will be agreed upon for election in the primaries.

* Since writing the above, the election of John J. O'Brien, as temporary chairman of the new organization, makes the fact patent to every one, that the old bosses are still in command.—Our politics are now: O'Brien *vs.* Kelly.

X.

REPRESENTATION AND SELF-GOVERNMENT FOR INHABITANTS OF CITIES.

WE have now seen that the origin and growth of Germanic civilization has been through the union or groups of men with the same material interests; that the New England township was a model rural group of that character; that the Fathers who formed our Constitution, intended to form a government in which these groups of farmers, with their material interests, should be fairly represented; that since then large groups of men have appeared, who gain their living not from the soil, but from working its detached products, and who consequently can live in great masses, in cities; that no attempt has been made to give to these inhabitants of cities, thus grouped according to their material interests, representation or self-government, that the subject of city government has never received thorough scientific consideration; that our city governments are formed after models of those introduced by the Stuarts, for the purpose of destroying popular government, by keeping the citizens disorganized in geographical election districts; that these governments fail to give satisfaction, wherever they exist, because citizens lack self-government and representation; that all attempts at improvement have failed, and that no real hope of improvement is held out by any prominent writer. May we not then draw the conclusion that, since men living in cities are not essentially different from those living in the country, they feel the same need to rally around their vital interests, *i. e.*, their means of gaining a living, and protect these interests from interference by outsiders, and from injury by dishonest fellow-workmen; in other words, the trade, business and professional organizations need, and before long will surely have representation in our city, state and national legislatures, and more or less self-government and control over their own members, after the model of the rural associations, called townships,

The object of representative government is to secure consideration and, so far as possible, realization of the wills of the inhabitants, and, since all cannot attend the legislative meetings in large states, a small number of representatives must act for the people.

Men have an infinite number of wishes, hence it is impossible to have all the wishes of all the inhabitants represented, and we must be content to have their strongest wishes represented. To secure this, men must first be united in groups, with strong wishes in common, and when these unions are represented, the most important interests of the people are represented. That men's strongest interests centre around their means of gaining a living, in their business, trades, professions, or as managers of their property, needs no argument in this busy city of New York.

There ought to be no broad distinction between our public and private affairs. If an individual or a number of individuals wish to send an agent to transact any business with others, the first care is to choose a man who has no other interest than theirs. The wisdom of this principle is so well established that our law, for example, will not allow an agent, employed to sell a thing, to become the purchaser, under any circumstances; no man can serve two masters.

Only by having men with the same most important interests united and presented, can we have real representative government. Our present representatives understand the wishes of their constituents about as well as the person who is "it," in the children's game of shouting proverbs.

Since, therefore, the participation of these organizations appears to be theoretically in accordance with the spirit of our Germanic institutions, and the legitimate development of the principles of the authors of our Constitution, I think it can be shown with equal certainty that we will derive direct, practical benefits from allowing these trade, business and professional organizations the right of representation and a certain amount of self-government.

XI.

PRACTICAL BENEFITS FROM REPRESENTATION OF CITIZENS, ORGANIZED ACCORDING TO THEIR INTERESTS.

BY allowing them representation, we will be benefited as individuals, as members of these organizations and as members of the State.

In the first place, our rights as individuals are not properly protected by our so-called representatives, because they, as a rule, are not up to the general moral and intellectual standard of the average citizen.

When men come together in an election district to make political nominations, the man having the most extensive personal acquaintance will surely control the meeting.

Hard-working trade, business, or professional men, as a rule, have but few acquaintances in their election district; the year has not evenings enough to enable them to get a real acquaintance with their fellow-voters, if they were to devote themselves to the task, especially if we consider how often our citizens move from one district to the other, and also the many social difficulties which would inevitably ensue from such an attempt. The only class, which can acquire such a local acquaintance is the small retail trader, especially the liquor dealer, hence their prominence in our government.

By hypocritical professions of interest and friendship with the large number of men, generally not of the best character in their neighborhood, with whom their business naturally brings them in contact, and by the dispensation of cheap, but highly prized favors to the most needy, these liquor-dealers wield and will continue to wield great influence in our government.

But it is self-evident that these men, and the professional politicians, which they become, if sufficiently adroit, do not possess the same sterling qualities of heart and head as the average hard working man engaged in commercial, trade, mechanical or professional pursuits. On the other hand, experience shows that delegates from business, trade and professional organizations are not blatant demagogues, but that sober, hard-working, conscientious, and able men can alone gain the esteem and confidence of their brethren in business or trade; such men would not have repeatedly passed the Penal Code, with reading only its first and last sections. Such men will better protect our so-called natural rights of life, limb, liberty and property, than ward politicians and leaders of "deestricks." The last report of the political committee of the Union League Club recognized this, when it recommended that the government of this city had better be left with the Legislature at Albany, than entrusted to our own delegates, for they evidently preferred to trust to the general honesty of the men elected by the associations of farmers, than to our own representatives, elected according to our present system.

Secondly, such men will also protect our rights as members of the various organizations; and since the interest of a city consists only in the aggregate of the important interests of its citizens, and since the important interest of the City of New York is its commerce and trade, everything done to foster and protect our commerce will tend to the welfare of the city.

Each man will, of course, have the interest of his own association most at heart, like the men from country districts. But all professions and trades recognize the fact that their business depends for its success on the city's commercial prosperity.

But our present representatives do not represent any of these important interests. No legislation ever affects directly or exclusively their "deestrick;" the members of the different trades and professions live scattered throughout the city, so that they form but an insufficient part of the constituency of any one delegate, and he need care but little for their opinion, especially if there happen to be residents in the district with more or less conflicting interests. Thus an important interest may send several representatives, because its members live together in a few districts, while other more important interests may not be represented, because the men live scattered in many districts; this is perhaps one of the causes why the pilots are able to maintain their tax on the commerce of the City of New York.

Even questions that affect a given locality do not always receive attention; for example, in the case of a recent attempt to remove a conceded nuisance—in which I acted as counsel—our representatives took little interest, because it was soon discovered that the diverging wants of tenants and property owners allowed them to act only to a certain extent in concert. Moreover, our city, as the commercial centre, will always have certain interests, to a certain extent, in opposition to those of the remainder of the State, the representatives of our geographical election districts do not duly assert them; witness, for example, the fact that every year hundreds of thousands of dollars raised by taxation from this city are spent for educational purposes in other parts of the State. The recent freedom of the Erie Canal would, moreover, never have been gained by our city representatives; their indifference was equalled only by the hostility shown to the construction of that canal by the Tammany Hall buck-tail politician of that day.

The presence of these delegates, watching over the business and trade interests of the City of New York, will, therefore, be of benefit to all engaged in trade, business or professional life. There was a deep meaning in the words of Governor Cleveland, on Evacuation Day: "Are you sure that you have in your legislative halls proper champions of the cause of your commerce? Are you sure you have the proper men at Albany to guard your precious interests? . . . You must not forget that your political interests go hand in hand with your commercial interests." Lastly, the representation of such organizations will be of benefit to the whole State, whose prosperity is so closely connected with that of this city, not only in the national legislature, where our representatives, elected on the same vicious principle, equally fail to protect our commercial interests, but also in the Legislature at Albany, where the representatives of the agricultural interests feel the want of a corresponding representation of our great State's commerce, to enable them to decide rightly the many complicated questions affecting special commercial interests.

Our best city representatives are young lawyers, but even these bring with them, as a rule, little or no acquaintance with these wants of business men; hence by affording the Government reliable means of gaining information on these commercial questions, which are continually increasing in importance and difficulty, you are rendering a service to the whole State. Congress has to appoint special committees which, at great expense, travel through the land and gather information, which instructs, to a certain extent, the members of that committee; but, with their retirement from office, the work has to be repeated.

Our State Legislature, occasionally, goes through a similar form, but its term of office is far too short to thus get any real knowledge.

As Governor Seymour has rightly said, our country has been governed by the statesmanship of the plough; however, not only is this Government naturally inclined to be also a little too much *for* the plough, but, for the sake of the farmers as well as for the city people, there should be a little more statesmanship of the workshop and of the desk.

In the words of John Stuart Mill, in his "Representative Government" (p. 65): "Each is the only safe guardian of his own rights and interests"; and again, on page 170: "No class, not even the most numerous, shall be able to reduce all but itself to political insignificance."

Of course, the objection will be raised that this is only the old guild-system, which has been tried and found wanting generations ago. But, in speaking of the guild-system, we should remember that it had two periods: the first when all were welcome who had necessary skill, and when it built cities, subdued robber knights, made the highways safe by land and by sea, extended commerce, patronized art, founded hospitals, built cathedrals:

> "I gaze round on the windows, pride of France,
> Each the bright gift of some mechanic guild
> Who loved their city, and thought gold well spent
> To make her beautiful with piety."—*Lowell's "Cathedral."*

As Lieber says, in his "Political Ethics": "Without them [the guilds] the cities would never have performed their high service in the promotion of civilization and the acknowledgment of the burghers' rights. (II., 199.)—The second stage when, as a close corporation, it enforced monopolies, crushed trade, and was used merely as an instrument of gain by the fortunate families who belonged to it—utterly regardless of the welfare of the rest of the citizens, and of the duties which were to be rendered in return for its rights. What caused this change?"

The same event which produced the same selfish and narrow spirit in all other European governments, after the fifteenth century, and, in fact, caused in all respects the greatest injury to our Germanic civilization. I mean the Renaissance.

That introduced the old heathen spirit of selfishness; no power would recognize any other in the State; it turned royalty into absolute monarchy, feudal chiefs into petty sovereigns, republics into close tyrannical corporations; it abolished all organizations intermediate between the State and the individuals, and left the latter as powerless atoms. The rural republics of Switzerland were as tyrannical as the guilds of the Hanse Cities; from the experience of that age we might as well argue against the agricultural township, as against the association of trade, professional and business men. The dislike against the exclusiveness of the old guild-system was justified; but we have let this dislike carry us too far; we have pulled down too much, and must now rebuild, but not with the old defects—the State must be supreme,

In fact, by this plan as to representation, we will have approached, as nearly as we can, to the ideal of Governor Seymour: "That government is most wise which is in the hands of those best informed about the particular questions on which they legislate; most economical and honest when controlled by those most interested in preserving frugality and virtue; most strong when it only exercises authority which is beneficial in its action to the governed." The helplessness of Congress, in dealing with such questions as that of the tariff, is universally acknowledged.

At present, only our wishes as individuals, or as members of the State at large, find utterance, such as it is, in our legislatures, in accordance with the theories of Aristotle and Rousseau; but our wishes, as members of organizations, between the State and the individual, are disregarded; though the interests of these intermediate associations of citizens, gaining a livelihood by similar means, are of the first importance; they deserve to rank with the townships and counties, as of equal birth with the state and national organizations; their importance is being recognized and insisted on by the so-called Professorial Socialists of Germany. The most oppressive and important function of government, *i. e.*, taxation, bears upon men, directly or indirectly, as members of these organizations; these organizations are at present not represented, and "taxation without representation is tyranny."

XII.

PRACTICAL BENEFITS OF SELF-GOVERNMENT OF CITIZENS ORGANIZED ACCORDING TO THEIR INTERESTS.

FINALLY, as to allowing these associations a certain amount of self-government, after the example of agricultural townships, it is, of course, impossible to lay down a general plan, but each association must be left to discover, by experience, to what extent it is capable and desirous of assuming such functions.

As to the necessity of not leaving these hundreds of thousands of inhabitants of cities without some form of sub-divisions with authority, there can be no question; the present local divisions of ward or election districts amount to nothing; they do not replace the "neighborhoods" of country; the only other possible organization to whom power can be entrusted, seems to be that of men united according to their material interests.

In the words of Professor Gneist, in his above cited article on the government of the City of London: "Is it possible to preserve the union of the neighborhood, where during the day and during the night a different population lives? It is natural that a people who find no longer support, help, sympathy in the neighborhood, should cling to the associations, which once existed as guilds, where the union of the neighborhood did not exist, and the important want could not be replaced by a periodical bringing together of unconnected masses of voters."

As Dr. Vaughan writes in his "Age of Great Cities:" "We are done with feudal restraints, but have adopted no others" (p. 283).

The great necessity is to replace this neighborhood influence; men lose in intelligence and in morals when they live only as individuals and atoms; that is a life for savages; they have no associations.

It is true that membership in these associations to some extent curtails our liberty and action; but these actions will, I believe, generally be found to spring from wishes, which it is well to limit. On the other hand the power of the individul is greatly increased through the association.

No honest business, trade or professional man in this city but feels the injury caused to his business or good name of his profession by the tricks and rascality of dishonest men in the same occupation, and who will not wish that there was some way of punishing this dishonesty, other than the expensive, often impracticable resort, to the State courts. Every trade or profession has regulations concerning the education and control of apprentices, the manner of doing work, etc., which it would wish to be able to put in force.

Every group of business men, mechanics or tradesmen acknowledges an obligation to assist a member of the same group, when disabled by age or misfortune. Are these not the same wants for whose satisfaction the farmers formed the much-lauded township governments?

The State does not know how to devise remedies for these wants of inhabitants of cities, or how to execute the remedies devised, any more than a centralized government can properly build and manage the necessary public institutions of all the villages and townships of the land.

All the indirect advantages which De Tocqueville and subsequent writers have represented as coming to the members of the township, from the habit of participating in self-government, will certainly also flow from membership in these associations of citizens. The inhabitant of the city thereby becomes a member of the body politic; he has a feeling of his strength, as a member in good standing of his business organization, and at the same time he feels the reponsibility of participating in great undertakings. By the periodical meetings with others of his business, trade and profession, where the best men in their respective lines are sure to take the lead, he sees a prize offered for honesty and excellence in his work, whatever that may be, and the punishment of social ostracism inflicted for the slightest breach of professional or trade morals. By contact with others leading a similar life, mutual friendships spring up; thence come confidence between man and man, that indispensable medium for business of any kind, that most important legal tender; thence comes the feeling of security that even in adversity there are friends on whom to rely; and last, but not least, comes a religious spirit, not a superstitous fear (for that is the result of helpless individualism of all savage or civilized life), but the trustful love of God, which follows the love of neighbor.

This improvement in morals and religion can be best brought about in this way, through the associations; clubs or churches for workingmen, gotten up expressly by churches or individuals will always be looked upon as charities and be attended so long as the material benefits are forthcoming; but these artificial structures will not last. Men of Germanic race require religion and its services as soon as they unite in associations; the object of our clergy should be, in the future, to work with and through those organizations; they may some day become parishes; each guild was formerly a religious unit.

And the benefits which men as individuals, as members of the general public, derive from the existence of these organizations, are as important as those of the members themselves. Every business and trade will only be too ready to discover and punish by expulsion from the trade or otherwise, all frauds or cheats; and thereby the public will be protected and the expense of many—generally unsatisfactory—lawsuits avoided, in the same way as, in the country, the opinion of the neighbors is the chief check on evil-minded persons.

By the benevolent mutual insurance system, which always comes sooner or later, the expense of supporting many aged and infirm persons will be taken from the State. Davis, in his standard English work on the Law of Friendly Societies, has remarked that trades-unions, by their benevolent institutions, perform many of the duties of the old parish, in helping those who are in want; they can manage a superannuation fund especially well, because they know when a man really cannot work; and also because many men entitled to "benefit" do not claim it, out of proper pride.

The good results to the public from the improvement in morals, by the saving of police-courts of justice and prisons, are obvious, and the sweeping penalties of the Penal Code—the only remedy of liberalism—will be done away with; but, especially important is the protection which these associations, by satisfying man's legitimate appetite for sympathy and co-operation, give society against the designs of communistic dreamers, whose influence is the result of our so-called liberal theories of individualism, cut-throat competition, and *bellum omnium contra omnes*. The Germanic workingman, like the farmer, has the desire for associations, and when these are denied to him, by antiquated conspiracy laws—the highest products of the wisdom of the Manchester school—any demagogue can move him by striking this note, and depicting to him in glowing colors the pleasures to be gained from this forbidden fruit. In these organizations of workingmen, according to trades, the steady, able craftsman has their confidence; the workingmen are as ready as the property-owners to exclude tramps and loafers from the franchise; they echo the words of Lieber: "We seek for a criterion which will enable us to distinguish those who have a fair stake in the welfare of the State from those who have not." They know too well how any socialistic talk makes capital take wings, and that the management of large concerns is not a sinecure, which any one could fill.

The socialistic leaders in this city know well that their only chance is in breaking down the separate trade-organizations and in getting the workingmen together in organized masses, where the demagogues' tongues can have full swing. As the greatest German political economist, Roscher, says: "They [workingmen's associations] can in peaceful contention with organizations of their respective employers satisfy one of the chief wants of our centralizing-atomizing times, namely, the restoration of strong active organizations between the State and the individual."

Not less important is the protection which the Republic will get from these organizations of trade and business men against the designs of ambitious political bosses.

In the words of Lieber : " This uninstitutional multitude has no organization; it is, as I have stated, necessarily led by a few or one, and thus we meet in history with the invariable result, that virtually one man rules where absolute power of the people is believed to exist ;" and " Longevity [of nations] together with progressive liberty is obtained only by institutional liberty." (361). President Woolsey, writing on the same subject, says : " A country without them is like a land without mountains ; it is these that awaken a perpetual joy in the soul. But despotism generally dislikes institutions, because they have an independent existence, and thus resist arbitrary will." (p. 365.) To quote again Governor Seymour's article ; " The theory of self-government is not founded upon the idea that the people are necessarily virtuous and intelligent, but it attempts to distribute each particular power to those who have the greatest interest in its wise and faithful exercise."

We see, therefore, that not only will the members of these associations, as such, derive benefit from our endowing these organizations with certain functions of self-government, but all citizens, as members of the State at large, and the State itself will be benefited thereby. As Lieber says in his work " On Civil Liberty ": " Strike out from England or America this feature and principle [all pervading associative spirit] and they are no longer the same self-relying, energetic, indomitable, active people. The spirit of self-government would be gone" (p. 126).

XIII.

SIGNS OF THE TIMES.

I DO not pretend that this is the key to any Utopia, but only that it is a remedy, and, I believe, the only remedy for many evils which inhabitants of cities now suffer, and which are steadily on the increase; this plan, like any other, will have some evil consequences; liberty without the possibility of mistake and wrong is impossible. In the words of Hamilton; " It (the argument) goes to prove that no powers should be entrusted to any body of men, because they may be abused" (II. Ell. Deb., p. 267). Our citizens have long recognized intuitively that in these organizations of men with common interests lay their only chance of political salvation, and these associations have been taking upon themselves more and more duties and powers of self-government, and have been every year taking a more direct interest in legislation.

Any one can observe these signs of the times in the daily newspapers. The following three are a few of the many notices I have found within the last two weeks, indicating decided advance in the direction advocated by this essay:

TO WATCH LEGISLATIVE WORK.

"At a meeting of the representatives of various commercial bodies, yesterday, at the Maritime Exchange, a permanent organization was effected under the title of The Association of New York Exchanges on Legislation. The purpose of the association is "to promote such legislation or measures as are favored, and to oppose such as are disapproved, by the exchanges or commercial bodies embraced in this association." The officers were elected as follows: President, Robert B. Van Vleck; First Vice-President, George E. Moore; Second Vice-President, John E. Henry; Third Vice-President, Charles C. Lathrop; Secretary, James De Mandeville; Treasurer, J. H. Seymour. An Executive Committee of one from each Exchange was elected. The association then adjourned for one week."

AT THE LAST MEETING OF THE CHAMBER OF COMMERCE

Mr. William D. Marvel, Chairman of the Committee to which was referred the subject of a commercial treaty with Spain, reported in favor of requesting President Arthur to appoint a commission to meet with the Spanish Minister and arrange for a commercial treaty; the commission to consist of one member appointed as the representative of the President, one representing the Senate, one the House of Representatives, one the Chamber of Commerce, and one member as the representative of the Maritime Association of this city.

PREPARING A BUILDING LAW.

The difference between the architects and builders on the one side and Inspector W. P. Esterbrook, the Mechanics and Traders' Exchange, and the Iron Founders' Association on the other side, last winter, which operated in the practical defeat of the proposed building law, introduced into the Senate by Senator Browning, on February 12, have apparently been harmonized this season. Mr. Esterbrook extended an invitation recently to gentlemen representing the New York Chapter of the American Institute of Architects, the Architectural Iron Manufacturers' Society, the Mechanics and Traders' Exchange, and the Real Estate Owners and Builders' Association to meet him and prepare a new bill, which all could unite in supporting. In pursuance to the invitation, a meeting was held in the Ashland House, last Tuesday evening, and a joint committee from the various organizations was appointed. It met at the Ashland House last evening and began the work of revision. The defeated bill was taken up and its sections discussed and remodeled. This work will not be completed for several weeks, but it is not expected that any great alterations will be made in it.

The new Real Estate Exchange, consisting of leading brokers and large real estate dealers in this city, according to an interview published in to-day's *Real Estate Record*, intends to take an active part in securing legislation necessary for the interests of property owners in this city, and especially with regard to reform in the law of land transfers; the *Record* insists that governments do not do it.

And here I would remark that what I have stated with reference to organizations of men, with common business, trade or professional interests applies equally to organizations of property owners. They, too, have interests to be represented and are entitled to self-government, for the protection of their special interests; they would continue to be organized according to geographical districts. Their interests do not coincide with their tenants, as was shown in the instance which I have above cited, of an attempt to remove a railroad nuisance from the West Side of this city; both tenants and property owners worked together at first, so as to have the nuisance diminished, but the tenants soon recognized that, if the nuisance were removed, the character of the neighborhood would be changed, the property would become more valuable and they would be forced to move, hence they lost interest and practically did not object to the lukewarmness of their representatives in the matter.

This is an example of the present helplessness of property owners against illegal acts, if so great as to affect the character of the neighborhood,

Politicians are recognizing this coming power; there is no shrewder man among them than Gen. James Husted, and this is a specimen of the sentiments which he has recently repeatedly uttered :

"Mr. Hooley is the President of the Working Men's Assembly, which will meet in this city in a few days. His indorsement of the bill is sufficient for me," said Mr. Husted, "and I follow where he leads." There was no further opposition, and the bill was ordered to have its third reading to-morrow. The Commission is required to bring in a bill in support of whatever conclusion it reaches. The five Commissioners will be paid $10 a day.''

The Utica Assembly of Trades last year nominated and elected an Assemblyman.

In fact, everything shows that the same thing is going to happen, which has always happened where men of Germanic race have been allowed to form their own governments; that they will not be satisfied to exist as disorganized masses, but will unite in defence of their interests.

XIV.

PRACTICAL SUGGESTIONS.

NO legislation is needed, at least for the present; a too hasty recognition of the public rights and duties of these organizations might lead to as unfortunate consequences as the present system. The organizations are forming themselves and assuming new duties rapidly; although citizens might be encouraged to join themselves to these associations, if they received some legal recognition, such as some slight power to prevent dishonesty, in their various callings.

What we should do now is this: This coming change in our form of government should be recognized, its causes studied, its progress foreseen, so that the transition to the new state of things may be as easy and tranquil as possible. The great danger is that some strong interest or group of interests will endeavor to gain for themselves the right of representation and self-government to the exclusion of other groups, with equal rights to these privileges; for example, by the plan of confining the ballot to real estate owners. That has been the trouble heretofore with Germanic cities, that one group would try to assert itself to the exclusion of others.

The same problem was solved by the authors of our Constitution, by the institution of two chambers, in one of which all interests should be equally represented, as such, and in the other the inhabitants should be represented according to numbers. The conflicting interests of organizations of farmers living in very different climates, fully as various as the trades in our cities, were thereby

harmonized, and the plan worked well, even after the
injurious influences of representatives, elected from our
city geographical election districts, made themselves felt;
and on this model, I believe, an Alliance of Business,
Trade, Professional and Property-Owners' Associations of
the City of New York might be formed, which would
secure us self-government and real representation, at first
perhaps indirectly, by exercising a pressure upon the
potitical parties, by endorsing or rejecting nominations,
but before long by making nominations, and finally by
becoming themselves the political units, in place of the
present geographical election district, which is unscientific
in theory, unjustified by history and condemned by
experience.

A constitution in outline, for such an Alliance, is
hereto annexed. Citizens, all over the city, would vote
for the nominees of this association, and thus we would
begin by carrying out practically Mr. Hare's plan, so
warmly endorsed by Mr. Mill in his "Representative
Government," with the exception that we would have
added the indispensable nominating committee, in which
the interests of all citizens might be represented. And,
in conclusion, I would venture to suggest that an association of men interested in this question might at once be
formed to study this movement in all its bearings in the
past and in the present, to collect facts showing the
tendencies of the movement in different localities, and to
oppose the attempts of the professional politicians to gain
control of the associations, and use them for selfish purposes, especially by antagonizing them, and to diffuse
among the members of these organizations an appreciation of their great usefulness and of their important
future.

By thus helping to organize the great masses in our
cities, and giving them representation and self-govern-

ment, we would be carrying out the true principles of our Germanic Constitution, and doing our share towards hastening the fulfilment of Hamilton's prophecy:

"The time may ere long arrive when the minds of men will be prepared to make an effort to *recover* the Constitution."

The need of the hour is a new federalism.

CONSTITUTION OF THE ALLIANCE

OF THE

Trade, Professional and Property-Owners' Organizations

OF

NEW YORK CITY.

Section 1.

The object of this Alliance is to promote the interests of the inhabitants of the City of New York, by securing for them the rights of representation and self-government.

Section 2.

The Alliance shall consist of delegates from each of the associations, which shall sign this constitution, or which shall afterwards be admitted to this Alliance.

Section 3.

Each of said associations shall appoint three delegates; this appointment shall be made before the close of the year, for the ensuing year; such appointment shall be witnessed by a certificate, signed by the secretary and sealed with the seal of the association.

Section 4.

The officers of this Alliance shall be a President, two Vice-Presidents, a Secretary and a Treasurer, who shall be elected at the first regular meeting of the Alliance, and hereafter at the last regular meeting of each year, and shall hold office for one year, and perform the usual duties of their respective offices; no two of said officers shall be members of the same association, but this latter rule shall not apply to the secretary.

Section 5.

The following committees and all others, authorized by the by-laws, shall be appointed by the president; and each committee shall consist of three members, except the Executive Committee, which shall consist of one member from each of the associations.

Section 6.

The Committee on National Legislation, the Committee on State Legislation and the Committe on Municipal Legislation shall keep themselves informed concerning legislation, in the national, state or municipal legislative bodies respectively, and shall also keep a record of votes by the members of those bodies on matters of importance to this Alliance.

Section 7.

The Committee on Business Organizations shall keep itself informed concerning business organizations, not members of this Alliance, and shall seek to gain their co-operation, and to diffuse among their members an appreciation of the benefits to be derived by self-government and representation of such organizations.

Section 8.

The Committee on Arbitration shall act as arbitrators in disputes between associations who are members of this Alliance (if any should arise), and the members of said committee shall also act as arbitrators in disputes between members of different associations, and may also accept such compensation as may be agreed upon by all parties for such services.

SECTION 9.

The Committee on Legislation shall consider all proposals for amendment of the law.

SECTION 10.

The Committee on Nominations shall consider nominations for public offices, made by political parties, and shall recommend to the Alliance the endorsement or rejection of such nominations, or shall suggest that nominations be made by the Alliance.

SECTION 11.

The Committee on Grievances shall conduct such litigation as may be directed by the Alliance; but no suit shall be begun except when authorized by three-fourths of the associations.

SECTION 12.

The Committee on Self-Government shall keep itself informed concerning the relations of the various associations to their members, and, when appealed to, shall recommend such action as shall seem conducive to the best interests of all parties.

SECTION 13.

The Committee on Membership shall consider all applications for membership from other associations.

SECTION 14.

The annual dues of each association shall be ———— dollars, to be paid in the month of January; further expense shall be borne equally by the associations, but none shall be authorized except by a vote of **three-fourths** of the associations.

SECTION 15.

Each delegate shall be entitled to one vote, and plurality of votes shall decide all questions, except where the constitution requires a vote of associations; in such cases each association, represented at the meeting, shall have one vote, to be cast by a majority of its delegates; if only two delegates of any association are present and cannot agree, the vote of that association shall not be counted; and if only one delegate is present, he can vote for the association.

SECTION 16.

New associations may be admitted, and the constitution may be amended by a vote of three-fourths of the associations; but any member, proposing such admission or amendment, shall give notice thereof to the secretary, at least one week before the monthly meeting, and the secretary shall immediately give notice thereof to the members of the Alliance, in the manner provided for calling special meetings.

Federalism and the Social Contract Theory.

THE characteristic which lies at the foundation of Federalism and distinguishes it in all times from other systems of government is the belief in the existence of absolute principles of right and wrong, which were created by God and which exist independently of the human reason.

By the desire to realize these higher ideas, men are led to form governments; as the Federalist says, on page 364 (Dawson's Ed.): "Justice is the end of government. It is the end of all civil society."

Moreover, believing that human reason may not always recognize these great truths, and in order to hand them down to posterity, Federalism imbeds them in constitutions beyond the reach of the transient whims of a bare majority of the multitude.

Thus the preamble of our Constitution reads: "We, the people of the United States, in order to form a more perfect union, establish justice . . . and secure the blessings of liberty to ourselves and our posterity, do ordain and establish this Constitution for the United States of America."

To quote again from the Federalist (p. 498): "It (the republican principle) does not require an unqualified complaisance to every sudden breeze of passion, or to every transient impulse which the people may receive from the arts of men, who flatter their prejudices to betray their interests."

On the other hand, Federalism does not place the individual helpless in the hands of an almighty government, but maintains numerous organizations between the individual and the State. Thus the Federalist says (p. 56): "From this view of the subject, it may be concluded, that a pure democracy, by which I mean a society consisting of a small number of citizens, who assemble and administer the government in person, can admit of no cure for the mischiefs of faction;" and again, on p. 235: "The Federal and State governments are in fact but different agents and trustees of the people, constituted with different powers and designated for different purposes." Our towns, counties and states were unions of agriculturists, each of which managed its own affairs, and whose representatives met together to reconcile their conflicting interests and protect themselves from others.

In political economy, Federalism is, in the first place, opposed to Communism. In the words of the Federalist: "The diversity in the faculties of men, from which the rights of property originate, is not less an insuperable obstacle to a uniformity of interests. The protection of these faculties is the first object of government. From the protection of different and unequal faculties of acquiring property, the possession of different degrees and kinds of property immediately results; and from the influence of these on the sentiments and views of the respective proprietors ensues a division of the society into different interests and parties. The latent causes of faction are thus sown in the nature of man." (p. 57.) "Among the numerous advantages promised by a well-constructed union, none deserves to be more accurately developed than its tendency to break and control the violence of faction" (p. 55).

On the other hand the Federalist recognizes the right of every trade and occupation to maintain its separate interests; thus Letter 58 reads: "A landed interest, a manufacturing interest, a mercantile interest, with many lesser interests grow up of necessity in civilized nations. The regulation of these forms the principal task of modern legislation." The whole spirit of Federalism is opposed to permitting one class to oppress another at the expense of the physical and moral health of the latter. The founders of our government conceived its scope to extend beyond the exercise of a mere police power; the Constitution declares one of its objects to be "to promote the general welfare." Our population at that time was an agricultural one, and consequently the necessity for laws regulating the treatment of employees by employers were as little known as they are at present, for employees in our agricultural districts or for our household servants; but the apprenticeship and usury laws, and the provisions for building roads and public education, indicate that the Fathers placed no narrow bounds upon their idea of the duties of a State, or of the minor organizations.

Law, they held, is not confined to keeping the peace between individuals, or merely compelling them to fulfill contracts, but justifies the prohibition of any act which interferes with any of the greater or smaller organizations attaining the objects of their existence.

What theory in politics, political economy and law has been the great opponent of the doctrines of Federalism, as above set forth?

Luther Martin in his report to the Maryland Legislature (I. Elliott's Debates, p. 351), concerning the proceedings in the convention which framed the United States Constitution, states: "They (the opponents of the United States Constitution) urged that all men considered in a state of nature, before any government is formed, are equally free and independent, no one having any right or authority to exercise power over another, and this without any regard to difference in personal strength, understanding or wealth, and that when such individuals enter into government, they have each a right to an equal vote in every matter which relates to their government."

This language is that of the adherents of the social contract theory, which has continued to be the opponent of Federalism to the present day, and the object of this paper is to show the history of this political doctrine, together with a brief reference to its effects on political economy and law.

This theory, to state it briefly, is as follows: It assumes that men lived originally in a state of nature without laws or government, but that for various reasons they found this unendurable, and consequently, guided by their reason, they met and resolved to live in social relations and form a State, submitting themselves to an individual, or to a number of individuals, who hereby became their rulers.

The agreement to live in a State is called pactum unionis; the agreement to form a government is called pactum constitutionis; and the agreement between governors and governed is called pactum subjectionis. Of course no place is found for organizations intermediate between the State and the individuals. These are probably the only points on which all the various supporters of this theory agree. The influence of this theory was so widespread, that a reference to most of the prominent political writers will be necessary.

I.

But, before we go further into the history of its development, a short account should be given of the theories and causes which, apparently, led up to the adoption of this theory. Among the Greeks, the necessity of any explanation of the unlimited power of the Government does not seem to have been felt. Ulysses, when he chastises Thyrsites, that prototype of democratic demagogues, gives no explanation of why Agamemnon was entitled to such a large share of the spoil, and so many beautiful women, beyond the heavy weight of his staff. And, in later times, when the governments had become republics, there was no question but that the Government might do what it pleased. Thus, in the trial of the naval commanders, after the battle of Arginusæ, the law of procedure, which allowed only one man to be tried at a time, was changed, and the commanders were all tried at once; for, said the popular orators, if we, the people, decide on their fate, can we not also say how we will do it?

In the same spirit, Plato, in his republic, sacrifices the individual entirely to the State. He sacrifices the wellbeing of the individual; he seeks only a successful and splendid State, in which an individual must find his satisfaction in knowing that he belongs to it. Thus, he denies to the ruling class all private property; even their wives must be in common, so that no interests, other than the common welfare, may distract their attention; and, as to the condition of the lower class, consisting of the laborers, artisans, etc., nothing is said of their having any rights, or deserving any consideration.

Aristotle, whose ideas were intended more for real life, considered man as an animal, destined by nature to form a State. The object of the State is to live well; it may be in the form of monarchy, aristocracy or democracy, whichever is best suited to a city's particular circumstances. But, like Plato, he considers the individual as completely subordinate to the State, and does not consider that any question can be raised as to the origin or propriety of this relation.

The explanation of this may lie in the fact that the Greeks were then for the first time experiencing the advantages derived from city life, in which, necessarily, the central authority must be very great; their idea of a State was the city; the will of the citizens, who could meet easily, was naturally the supreme law; all the greatest goods seem to be gained only by this close cohesion of men and subordination of one to all; hence all small unions, such as trade-guilds and even families, were disregarded, and the immoderate extension of the principle of absolute government seems to have been one of the principal causes of the unsteadiness and final downfall of these cities and states.

Their philosophy had destroyed their old religious beliefs, but they had substituted no new system to carry up man's thoughts to God; they made man the centre of the universe and his reason or will his all-sufficient guide.

The Romans, as little as the Greeks, felt the need of any theory to account for the existence of the State. Their absolute public authority, which seems to resemble most nearly the strong power possessed by a robber chieftain over his band, was never decreased even when the conquest of the world had made it unnecessary. The only remedy they could think of was to increase the number of men who wielded this absolute power; thus two consuls were appointed in place of one king; and again later, two tribunes were installed to check the two consuls.

The Romans also copied all their theoretical ideas from

the Greeks; hence they repeated the teachings of the entire absorption of the individual into the State; although they were unconscious of the fact that the independence of the pater-familias in all matters pertaining to private law was in direct contradiction to the Greek spirit.

The Greek idea of the State, as a city, was also unfortunate for the Romans, as it prevented the adoption of any theory suitable to its world-wide government, which continued till the time of the absolute empire to be that of a city, governing a surrounding country; thus a civis romanus could exercise his privileges only in the City of Rome, etc.

To Christianity is due the elevation of the individual from being merely an instrument of the State; the high value set upon every man as possessing an immortal soul, raised the humblest individual above the greatest productions of this world.

St. Augustine thus considers the State only as a necessary evil, the work of the children of this world, with which it is better to have no more to do than is necessary. The real State is supernatual; it is the union of all true believers in the Church, and the earthly governments should serve only the ends of the Church, since they, like everything else, are the direct productions of the Lord.

Charlemagne and the succeeding emperors were considered as having the mission of realizing the heavenly kingdom so far as possible on this earth; hence their authority was deemed to be derived directly from God. The cry of " Deus vult " was the expression of an opinion on earthly matters not confined to the Crusades, but applicable to political institutions in general.

Dante is the chief writer of this period, and his Latin political writings are full of yearnings for unity under the German Emperor, who derived his authority through the Pope, from God; but the question of the origin of government is not raised; Aristotle, the "philosophus," said nothing about it, and that was enough.

Later writers followed in the same direction, bound by the authority of Aristotle and Thomas Aquinas; the former in worldly, the latter in spiritual matters, being the sufficient authority.

It was not until the sudden influx of new ideas into Western Europe, which followed the fall of Constantinople, had overturned the established ideas of the relations of God and man, that men began also in political matters to question the origin and authority of existing institutions.

This was, however, not done by the leaders of the Reformation; on the Continent, they recognized existing civil authority as an institution of God, although not so directly as had been heretofore assumed. The legal and moral duties of a man were derived from the decalogue, and Melancthon's moral philosophy treats of our rights and duties as arising directly from God's command.

They did not follow out, in political questions, the same course of investigation which they adopted in regard to Church matters, where they assumed by their reason alone to be able to discover at any time, without reference to past development, the true will of God.

II.

The first writer to claim a similar pre-eminence for human reason in political matters, appears to have been Hugo Grotius, in his work entitled "De jure belli et pacis," published in 1625.

His object was most laudable. He had seen the miseries which were produced by the unmitigated violence of the religious wars of that period; he could not appeal to the commands of God, as reason for their mitigation, because the contestants believed that they were fighting under God's commands, and that it was obeying Him and pleasing Him to destroy His enemies. Grotius, therefore, had to find some authority other than God. In chapter I. of his first book, he says: "That which we call Natural Right or the Law of Nature is the dictate of right Reason. . . . . The Law of Nature is so immutable that God himself cannot alter it." And in the introduction he bases the civil law on this natural law, as follows: "Again seeing that it is a dictate of the Law of Nature to fulfil covenants and agreements (for it is necessary that there should be some means of obliging men among themselves, nor can there be any other means found that is natural) from this spring flow all civil laws."

The state, therefore, arises from contract, contract arises from natural law and natural law arises from human reason, which would have binding authority, as he says in his preface, "though we should grant, what without great wickedness we cannot, that there is no God, or that He takes no care of human affairs."

Although Grotius thus derives the authority of the state from the people, his teachings were not revolutionary, because he considers the people as having transferred the authority inallenably to their sovereign; nor did he have much effect upon private law, because his attention was chiefly directed to international law, with which we need not concern ourselves in this essay. He merely refers to private law in his first chapter of first book as "that law that is of lesser extent, and ariseth not from the civil power, though subject unto it, is various, comprehending under it that of a father over his children, that of a master over his servants and the like." From this passage, one might conclude that he considered these legal institutions to have an origin independent of the public authority and the social contract; and the subsequent brief treatment of the institutions of private law in Chapter III. to V. of Book II. does not dispel this idea, although he treats of marriage as an institution of natural law; he does not consider individuals as having transferred all their rights to the state, but only such as are necessary for the common defence.

The reason why Grotius and his successors on the continent adopted the theory of contract, as an explanation of the origin of government, is that at that time, owing to peculiar historical reasons, the mere agreement of the parties (*nudum pactum*) had become actionable. The Roman law, as is well known, considered an agreement to be actionable only in case it was in the form of a stipulatio, or in case something was delivered or performed (real contract), except in the four cases of sale, lease, mandate and partnership, in which the mere consent of the parties sufficed.

In the old Germanic law on the continent, a similar rule had prevailed, that mere agreements were not actionable; thus, in our English law, bonds and covenants corresponded to the Roman stipulatio, and our old doctrine of consideration, which did not consider a promise a good consideration for a promise, made the cases in which informal promises were actionable correspond very nearly to the real contracts of the Roman law.

However, by the reception of the Roman law on the continent, the old Germanic forms, in which a promise had to be clothed in order to be actionable, were pushed aside, and as the Roman forms were unsuited to Germanic modes of life and business dealings, they were not adopted nor did any new forms spring up so that the principle that the *nudum pactum* was actionable, which the Romans had particularly confined to the above mentioned four contracts, was generally adopted for the first time, probably in the history of an Aryan people.

Another fact, which tended to produce the idea of the inherent binding power of a promise, was the weight which the Church had through all the middle ages laid upon the solemnity of an oath. The Church carried this so far as to insist that the benefit of all laws passed for the protection of an individual or of a class, might be waived by an oath to that effect; for, they said, a broken oath will send a man's soul to hell, which far exceeds any earthly ill which he might suffer. Hence, minors were allowed to make binding contracts, if they swore that they would not resist payment by appealing to the law, which prohibited their making contracts.

The remains of the spirit of chivalry, also, were consonant with this idea, that all promises raised binding obligations, for breach of his plighted word was one of the worst offenses of which a knight could be guilty; so that enemies were in the habit of releasing each other on parole, so soon as the amount of the ransom had been agreed upon. It appears, therefore, that all of the three ruling castes of that age—the lawyers, the clergy and the knights, were familiar with the idea that all promises must be kept, and that it would have been against all their teachings and prejudices to have questioned it.

The material situation of the mass of the people at that time had also much to do with the wide influences which this theory obtained. One of the many evil consequences which the sudden immense influx of new ideas, known as the Renaissance, brought with it—in consequence of the inability of one age to digest and assimilate so vast an amount of new facts and theories—was that the feudal chieftain assumed all the privileges and absolute powers of the rulers of the Greek and Roman states, and forgot all the duties which he owed to his vassals under the real feudal system, and which the more settled state of the country rendered less necessary.

Everywhere, therefore, at that time the rulers had been increasing their power and rights at the expense of their subordinates.

These rulers needed a theory by which to secure and justify their acquired rights, and the un-Germanic idea of one absolute corporation forming the state. This was furnished them by the social contract, which, as taught before Rousseau, led to the conclusion that the original contract between governors and governed once having been made, it could not now be altered, but was binding as any civil contract. The necessity for this artificial explanation arose, therefore, from the fact that the Greek and Roman forms of government were being forced upon a Germanic people. When a people has a suitable government it asks for no explanation of it. But the rulers of that century little thought that by the fostering of this artificial theory they were preparing a weapon which could be turned with equal force against their own pretensions.

Puffendorf in his book, "De Jure Naturæ" (1672), and "De Officio Hominis et Civis" (1693), developed Grotius' theory and applied it to all the institutions of private law, and he has been followed so blindly, as I will try to show hereafter, that he might almost be called the father of modern jurisprudence, although in his "De Jure Naturæ" he expressly disclaims the intention of writing a complete legal text book. He says: "So we that profess in this work to treat only of those duties of men which the light of reason shows to be necessary do not at all pretend that there ever was or now is or ought to be such a state in which those obligations only should prevail, exclusive of all others." Puffendorf was not a great original thinker; his ideas were chiefly derived from or suggested by Grotius and Hobbes (whom we shall consider later); but he first treated all legal relations from this standpoint of natural law, and hence his book had such a widespread influence. He confuses law and morals; he breaks off the slender band which Grotius still maintained between God and man, and declares the latter's reason to be all sufficient; he founds the institution of marriage upon the consent of the parties, and makes desperate efforts to discover some implied consent to explain the duties of parent and child. Property of individuals is derived from all things having been originally held in common, and this communism would be the proper condition of things, except where, by the terms of the social compact, occupation is allowed. Torts and crimes and all subjects which could not be explained as contracts, were pushed into the background.

Grotius and Puffendorf may, therefore, be considered the chief of the older exponents of the social contract.

As above stated, Puffendorf derived many of his ideas from Hobbes; but the latter cannot properly be said to have believed in the social contract. As an Englishman he knew that promises, unless in the form of a bond or covenant, were not actionable; thus, in Chapter XIV. of his Leviathan (published in 1651) he says: "Bonds that have their strength not from their own nature (for nothing is more easily broken than a man's word), but from fear of some evil consequences upon the rupture." He therefore derived the necessity of keeping the social contract merely from fear of what would happen if it were broken and men were left to their evil passions. He was led to this idea from contemplation of the disorders which filled England during the time of the Commonwealth.

In other points, however, his strong mind carried out the ideas of Grotius to their furthest consequences. His views on the state are well shown in his first introduction to the Leviathan: "For by art is created that great leviathan called a commonwealth or state (in latin, *civitas*), which is but an artificial man, ... and in which the sovereignty is an artificial soul, as giving life and motion to the whole body; . . . . lastly, the pacts and covenants by which the parts of this body politique were first made . . . . resemble that fiat or 'let us make man,' pronounced by God in the creation." From this we see that he considered the government absolute, and that men could create any form of it they pleased, which opinion he frequently reasserts. He recognized no other wrong than breach of contract.

Thus, in Chapter XV., he says: "And the definition of injustice is no other than the not-performance of covenant, and whatsoever is not unjust is just." In this opinion he goes further than Grotius or any of his successors. He derives the absolute power of government from proving, in Chapter XVIII., the absurdity of any other conclusion from the social contract, supposing that actually to have taken place. This mode of argument was subsequently to be applied to the theory to produce very different conclusions. This conclusion is expressed in Chapter XXI.: "Liberty of a subject lieth, therefore, only in those things which, in regulating their actions, the sovereign hath prætermitted."

He boldly carries Grotius' theory of the independence of man from God to its full extent; thus he says that atheism cannot be a vice, beause the atheist never submitted his will to God, and no one can have power over another except by the latter's consent. In this opinion he agreed with the absurd views of Spinoza, who declared that divine law began from that time when man by express compact promised to obey God in all things; by which deed they receded, as it were, from their natural liberty, and transferred their right upon God, just as sovereignty is conferred in civil states.

Kant was the next and last of the great writers who derived an absolute form of government from the social contract. The process of reasoning by which he reaches this conclusion is difficult to discover; thus, in his *Rechts-Lehre*, he says: "The legislative power can only belong to the united will of the people." But a few pages later he says: "Against the rightful head of the state there can, therefore, be no rightful resistance by the people." And: "The ruler in the state has towards his subjects only rights, not duties."

Judging from his general mode of philosophical argument, which assumes that things are not actually what they seem, but that they nevertheless exist in some ideal form, he probably considered that ideal and not real men made the social contract and instituted absolute government, concerning which subjects must not now indulge in presumptuous theories ("*Vernuenfleleien*"). Upon institutions of private law, however, he inconsequently still allows the *Volksmeinung* full play; thus, concerning the property of corporations, he writes in his *Anmerkung* A to his *Staats-Recht*: "So soon as this (*Volksmeinung*) ceases, and even if only in the opinion of those who by their merits have the pre-eminence. . . . . then the supposed right of property must also cease." The institution of the family, on the other hand, he regards as positive and unchanged, because demanded by reason.

We now come to the man who, starting with the same fiction of a social contract, came to very opposite conclusions from these supporters of absolute monarchies, which we have so far been considering. It was Jean Jaques Rousseau who captured this formidable battery of the ruling classes and trained its guns with such deadly effect upon its former owners. He accomplished this by the doctrine of inalienable rights, which he promulgated in his "Contrat Social." He adopted the theory of an original social contract without reserve; he says in Livre I., Chapter IV.: "Since no man has any natural authority over his equal, and since force produces no right, it follows that only contracts remain as a basis for all legitimate authority among men." He, however, differs in this from Grotius, in that he claims that there are certain rights of which men could not have disposed, because they could receive no equivalent; thus he says in Chapter IV., that for a freeman to sell himself would be absurd, because he could not be in his senses, since he could receive no equivalent for his liberty. He, therefore, in this respect, limits the power of man over himself.

Only one form of a good government is therefore possible, which consists in the complete transfer of all individual rights to the community, as a whole: "*enfin chacun se donnant a tous ne se donne à personne.*" (Liv. I., Ch. 6.) All individuals, therefore, are and remain equal, and a *volonté general* is created which is the sovereign, and in which all participate. He meets the objection that in a large state all citizens could not attend the assemblies, by suggesting that large states are not necessary, but each city may form a state by itself. (Liv. III., Ch. 13.) Like the Greeks and Romans and all his predecessors, he assumes that the power of this government, this *volonté general* is absolute over the individual.

The object is the *bien public*, which consists in all having an equal share of the goods of this world; hence, all other corporations except the state, and all individual interests must be abolished.

The officers of the government are the agents of the people, hence they are, at any time, liable to be called to account and deposed. This recall of power is no revolution, any more than a change of ministers by the king; rebellion is a thing which does not exist.

Rousseau had thus carried the theory of the social contract at one bound to the opposite extreme from that maintained by Hobbes and Kant. He had shown that it was absurd to claim that the original contract consisted in an entire renunciation of all rights on the part of the people, and that, if that had been the case, the contract was voidable. The supporters of monarchy could suggest no other theory than this social contract and had, therefore, to rely upon Hobbes' assertion that, if this contract were once broken, man would relapse into anarchy and barbarism.

It was the success and good order of our Revolution which knocked away this last prop of absolute monarchies. The New England descendants of the Puritans owed their freedom from the social contract theory, as well as many other of their peculiarities, to the fact that they had escaped the effects of the Renaissance. Their ancestors in England generally belonged to a class which was not affected by the Renaissance; and after their emigration to this country they were too busy with cutting down the forests and fighting Indians to think much of Grotius and Puffendorf. Besides, these theories of the supremacy of human reason contradicted their belief in the relation of God and man. They still considered themselves under the direct guidance of the Almighty, as all Europe did before the Renaissance; hence they set up their covenant with God, as their highest law. Hobbes calls this an unmanly lie; but, as a matter of fact, it was no more a lie than his fiction of the original contract; and at all events, it had the fortunate effect of preserving our people from its benumbing influence. The reason that New York was less ardent in the beginning of the Revolution may, in part, be ascribed to the fact that it was under the influence of a small number of wealthy families, who, by their superior means and more ample leisure, stood in more direct communication with the European thought of that day, and, like it, dreaded the consequences of questioning this theory, sanctioned by such high authorities.

Rousseau did not have to wait long for an answer; it was given him in the French Revolution, which, though brought about in a large part by the desire of realizing his Utopias, showed the utter incapacity of man to construct a state solely by aid of his reason; only the maddest of the mad, under Baboeuf, actually attempted to turn his ideal into reality, although his ideas were adopted in their repeated declarations of right.

II.

Since the French revolution the theory has lost its commanding position; the impracticability of its necessary consequences is recognized; in its entirety it serves now only as a convenient hypothesis on which some theoretician in law or political economy builds up an airy castle, with massive logic and unanswerable arguments; but its glittering generalities are still scattered through the books of many writers of note, and are still received as axioms, in apparent ignorance of their origin and necessary consequences; law and political science, especially, still suffer from the effects of its insidious poison, and languish, unaware of the chief cause of their disease.

But before I attempt to trace out the effects of this theory, in modern law and political economy, I would briefly here consider the merits of the social contract theory and show its fallacy as a theory and its effects on the public and private legal institutions of that age.

Of course, its great fault is that the whole thing never occurred; that the actual state was not formed from individuals, but from tribes, which again consisted of related families or from other smaller organizations; that the individual members of these tribes or other organizations were not living in a lawless state of nature, but under customary laws, which had been observed for ages; that the transition from a confederacy of tribes into a state was so gradual, that it probably had little or no effect upon the institutions of private law; that this transition was generally effected, not by the consent or promise of the individuals, but of the tribes or other organizations, which, as a rule, transferred only certain enumerated rights; that no organizations or individuals ever voluntarily surrendered absolute power over themselves and their property to any government.

When we consider these defects in the theory, which we would think would strike any superficial observer, we must wonder at the ascendancy which it gained, did we not have examples enough in our day of the influence which absurd theories can acquire when sanctioned by high authorities. When we see the real power which the theory still exercises and the weakness of the opposing theories, I think we will be less positive in this opinion.

The effect which this theory had in its days on public and private law was enormous. It first of all divorced all institutions, public and private, from all real connection with God; it failed, however, in all its attempts, to find a firm, new basis on which to erect them; for, since it was assumed that all institutions were invented by man, man must necessarily be able to change them at will; but, if man can make what institutions he pleases, he must also be able to give himself into slavery or into subjection to an absolute monarch. So that on the first theory any government might be overthrown at any time; but, on the second theory, no government, however oppressive, could be resisted or questioned. In the same manner all legal institutions were exposed to this uncertainty; even contract itself could not be shown to be binding; for, although I promised to do a thing, in the next minute I might refuse to perform it, as abridging my liberty. The right of property was denied by Proudhon on the same reasoning. Different writers attempted to avoid this dilemma by assuming that those rights which they approved of were inalienable, but the line was entirely arbitrary.

Not only the state, but all institutions were thus exposed to the popular whim. Thus marriage was not necessarily monogamous or a union for life; on the contrary, the freedom of man demanded that this contract might be dissolved at any time, at the will of either party, and certainly by mutual consent. The great fact that the community, as a whole, had any interest in the conduct of individuals, or any right to interfere with them, except where the individuals had consented to such right of interference, was denied. Hence, all legal institutions for which the ingenious imaginations of the philosophers could find no consent as its basis, were shriveled up or discarded altogether. Thus the rights and duties of parents and children towards each other formed a great stumbling block, which they could only partly get over by assuming that by the act of generation the parent had impliedly contracted to support his offspring; but the duty was reduced to a minimum, as this was felt to be a weak point.

The whole subject of civil wrongs or torts was usually omitted or brought in under the head of an implied consent, although it would seem that to hold a man liable for consent which he had never in fact given was as tyrannical as any act could well be. The subject of contracts was thereby divorced from that of torts and given undue importance and a separate treatment. Moreover, the whole subject of morals was introduced into law and mixed in inextricable confusion; the law of nature, as it was called, was considered as raising direct legal obligations, without further sanction by the legislative authority. In Germany, it is true, under the influence of Leibnitz, Thomasius distinguished legal from moral obligations by the criterion that only the former were to be enforced by the courts; but this distinction, as we will see hereafter, was not adopted by later English writers.

The precise and complete legal system of the Germanic lawyers was replaced, so far as possible, by a confused, barbarous jargon about natural rights, agreements, contracts, covenants, pacts, etc., which terms no two writers used in the same sense, or which often meant different things in the same volume or chapter. In England the Germanic law, under the name of the feudal system, was confined to the law of real estate, and could there keep up with the wants of national development only by laboriously defined fictions- which, however, were after all better than the fine sounding but utterly confused system which regulated personal property; the lawyers felt that the only salvation for the stability of the law of real property, on which such vast interests depended, was to keep it out of the vortex of natural law, which had swallowed so many legal institutions, and which necessarily led to communism.

Another, probably the most important, evil effect of the social contract theory was, as above stated, that all corporations or unions except the State must be abolished. Hobbes declared them to be the animalculæ which exist within and feed upon the human body, and Rousseau was most positive in his denunciations of them, because they intercepted the wills of the individuals, and kept them from forming that *volonté general* which was the only popular form of government. Other writers of this school were equally contemptuous of these intermediate organizations, or simply ignored them.

We will next endeavor to trace the influence of this theory upon the writings of the chief German philophers, and then, finally, upon the English and American writers on law and political economy. These men differ from the predecessors of Rousseau in this respect, that they did not actually believe that the social contract theory could be made a rule for the formation of the State, but they accepted it as a theory, in default of any other, to explain and justify the existence of government as a purely human institution without acknowledging God. Thus Fichte carried the theory of human independence to its furthest extent, identifying the thinking individual with the universe. In his "Natur-Recht" (page 139), he says: "The possibility of rights between individuals in natural law is based upon mutual trust and good faith;" and on page 129: "An original right is only a fiction, but it must be assumed for the purposes of science." No one carried the inevitable results of this theory more completely to their greatest extent; thus he says of property, on page 129: "The right to exclusive possession (property) is acquired by mutual consent, is limited by it, and cannot exist without it." He thus preached communism, pure and simple.

However, in his later work, entitled "Staats-Lehre," where he undertakes to construct an actual State, he follows a very different plan. To the question, "Who has the right to be ruler?" he replies, on page 87: "The highest human intelligence, and since this never exists, the highest intellect of that age and time." He then discusses at length how this highest intellect is to be recognized, and comes to the conclusion that the learned must name him as ruler from their midst who has shown the highest intellect. He, however, fails to explain how this aristocratic body of wise men is to form itself, and generally in his treatment of the subject seems to deserve the epithet of "ink-fish" which Schoppenhauer gave him, from the impenetrable cloud of words in which he enveloped himself.

A reaction against this whole social contract philosophy was started by Niebuhr's discovery of Gajus' manuscript, which had been written over with a homily of the Middle Ages. From this it appeared that the Roman law, and consequently the State, was not the product of pure reason and absolutely correct, but that it had undergone many and great changes. But the aversion to all philosophical theorizing on the subject of law was so great with Savigny and his followers that they never promulgated any definite system, but contented themselves with looking up the historical development of Roman law and studying out the meaning of dark passages in the corpus juris. And they then applied their conclusions, with but little respect for practical consequences, to upset long established ideas of Roman law, on which the most valuable rights depended.

To account for the rule of Roman law in Germany they generally compared the Roman law to Christianity, which had also spread from Rome and thus attempted to give Roman law a sort of halo, which should protect it from inquiry. The great growth of their school may be accounted for by its being in accordance with the popular sentiment at that time, which, sick of the social contract and the products of human reason, clung anxiously to all that had been handed down from the past.

But by the exaltation of the historical method, the Romanists raised an opposition historical school of the so-called Germanists, who contended that Germanic law should be the principal object of our research. They too, however, advanced no decided political or legal theory, being contented with the assertion that the chief source of law was custom, but they carefully and apparently intentionally avoided the natural conclusion that law was the will of the people. This would not have pleased the government, which supported the learned professors. However, the Germanists are gradually being forced to assume that popular customs of to-day also deserve attention, and under the theory of the so-called " Natur der Sache " they are beginning to recognise again the popular participation in the origin of law. Hegel in his Staats-Recht may be said to have developed the philosophy of this school, at least in its results as passively accepting existing governments. As the natural and inevitable result of history it is identical with the inferences to be drawn from the teachings of the historical school. As in his famous sentence: " What is rational (vernünftig) exists, and what exists is rational." He denied most emphatically the social contract theory, although the reason for the denial is somewhat strained; he says in §75: " The State must allow persons to enter and leave it; this is independent of the will of individuals, and the State therefore cannot rest on contract, because that requires free-will (willkur). It is incorrect to say that it depends on the will of all to form a State; it is on the contrary absolutely necessary for every one to be in the State." His extreme conservative tendencies are shown further by his denial in §273 of the right to alter the constitution, except in the manner provided for by the constitution. How he reaches his conclusions I would not dare to guess. As a specimen of his perspicacity I will cite his definiton of a State in §275: "The State is the reality of the moral idea—the moral spirit, as the revealed, self-conscious, substantial will, which thinks and knows and accomplishes that what it knows and so far as it knows it." Fortunately, however, he reassures us in §270: "The State exists in reality."

But in spite of this lack of clearness, Hegel deserves the greatest credit for having emancipated himself entirely from the social contract theory, and based the State upon the natural requirements of our being. The result of his writings has been to finally banish the social compact, even as a fiction, among the things of the past. I will only further call attention to Schleiermacher and Schoppenhauer, the former of whom seems to correspond with our utilitarian school and the latter with the later fatalistic and materialistic philosophy of Darwinism.

However, Schoppenhauer's abstract ideas of the origin of justice are of the highest value; but his practical conclusions, that the constitutional monarchy is the only natural form of government, is an evidence of the strength of his prejudices.

Ihering, probably the greatest of modern jurists, in his uncompleted work on "Zweck im Recht" (Purpose in Law), although in his earlier work on "Geist des Romischen Rechts" he adopted the social contract theory, promises to give us a philosophy of law equal in value to his preceding historical researches; in opposition to materialism, he insists upon the dependence of man on God, and that everything is not merely a means, but also serves a purpose. His work is one of the many signs that the world may in the not distant future draw not only its theory of government, but also its religion, from Germany.

We pass to a brief consideration of the influence which this theory had upon English writers on law and political theories. Its effect upon law cannot fully be traced in this essay, as it would lead us into a too technical discussion. I will only mention that the real origin of equity, as we have it to-day, dates from the time of Lord Nottingham, who became Chancellor under Charles II. We may safely assume that this sudden development of a few uncertain principles into the great fabric which arose at that time would not have taken place had not the writings of Grotius and Hobbes existed and shown the way to a larger adaptation of principles of morality as law. The first writers on equity are entirely under the influence of the social contract theory. However, the evils which accompanied this introduction of these teachings are very evident. A whole new terminology was introduced, so that the law of personal property, which came into importance since that time, has nothing to offer in comparison with the exact and complete system of the real estate law. All the evils, which I have before referred to as produced upon the Germanic laws of the Continent, were felt in England, although perhaps not to so great an extent, as the English were more practical in their nature; thus contracts received undue importance; duties arising from family relation were decreased; new duties to suit new forms of business were not imposed; the certainty of judgment of the older judges, as expressing the will of the people, founded upon absolute ideas of right and wrong, disappeared, and in its place came an anxious searching after some sort of an express or implied consent of the party to be charged with the duty. Blackstone wrote under the direct influence of Puffendorf and Hobbes, whom he cites frequently. His explanation of the origin of law and its definition is made up of inconsistent extracts from these writers, slightly modified by his practical knowledge of their absurdity.

Thus, although he denies that an actual social contract was ever made, nevertheless he assumes its existence as the chief argument against changing the British Constitution; he says in his introduction, section 2: "The Legislature would be changed from that which (upon the supposition of an original contract, either actual or implied,) is presumed to have been originally set up by the general consent and fundamental act of the society." Such a change, he implies, would produce anarchy, thereby placing himself on the standpoint of Kant as opposed to Rousseau.

Blackstone's further remarks about the law of nature, from which all human laws derive their authority, and which is to be recognized by individual reason, show the usual confusion of ideas of writers of that period, and fully deserve the merciless criticism to which they were subjected by Bentham in his "Fragment of Government." Unfortunately, Blackstone knew nothing of the work of Leibnitz and Thomasius, hence he mixes up law and morality in dire confusion; and still more unfortunately, no jurist has arisen in English law since his day to pull the English law out of the slough of despond into which the social contract theorists plunged it, as was done by Thomasius for continental jurisprudence.

The difference between Blackstone and Coke may be shown, for example, by the fact that Blackstone, in his third volume, derives the right to penalties from the original compact; but Coke, in the third part of his "Institutes" (chap. 69), says that a bond given to the king's officers to secure the performance of a public duty is void, "for that every man is bound to do to the king as to his liege lord all that appertaineth to him, without any manner of writing."

Bentham opposed this social contract theory with the theory of utility; he claims this in the historical preface to the second edition of the "Fragment of Government." But in fact he only takes up the opposite view to Blackstone, which Rousseau had promulgated, namely, that the government might be altered at any time by individuals; this in effect, of course, denied the binding force of the contract, and hence upset the theory. Thus he says, in chapter IV., page 37: "God forbid . . . . that in any society any convention is or can be made which shall have the effect of setting up an insuperable bar to that which the parties affected shall deem a reformation;" and again, on page 272: "Now, this other principle (for social contract theory) that still recurs upon us, what other can it be than the principle of utility? The principle which furnishes us with that *reason*, which alone depends not upon any higher reason, but which is itself the sole and all sufficient reason for every point of practice whatsoever."

"Utility" is, of course, nothing but another name for what we desire, what our reason leads us to desire; this is, therefore, only a translation of Rousseau's theory into English. Even the term "utility," which he claims to derive from Hume, occurs on the first page of the "Contrat Social," where Rousseau declares it to be his purpose "enfin que la justice et *l'utilité* ne se trouvent point devisés." Bentham's other great idea about the universality of law, that "the same arrangement that would serve for the jurisprudence of any one country would serve with little variation for that of any other" (introduction to "Fragment"), is common to all believers in the social contract and the infallibility of reason; and his theory of an absolute centralized government is evidently taken directly from Hobbes. Thus he says: "Have these supreme governors any such duties? No!" If Bentham had more often acknowledged the sources from which he drew his ideas, his theories would have had less weight, and his proposed changes would not have been so rashly adopted.

Austin, in his "Principles of Jurisprudence," although he most clearly shows the absurdity of claiming that an actual social contract was ever made, seems to place himself very nearly on the same standpoint as Hobbes, except that he also follows Bentham in adopting Rousseau's theory of inalienable rights. Thus, in the note on page 287, volume first, he says that Hobbes' capital errors are: Firstly, "He makes not the requisite allowance for the anomalous and excepted cases wherein disobedience is counselled by that very principle of utility which indicates the duty of submission." Secondly, "Instead of directly deriving the existence of political government from a perception by the bulk of the governed of its great and obvious expediency, he ascribes the origin of sovereignty and of independent political society to a fictitious agreement or covenant."

"Perception of expediency" and "utility" are, of course, only other names for the dictates of reason. Austin, also, retains the anti-Germanic notions of the supporters of the social contract theory concerning the necessity of an absolute "sovereign;" he quotes Grotius' and Hobbes' definitions of sovereignty as authorities, on pages 241 and 286; he follows Hobbes in the opinion that people obey government chiefly for fear of anarchy which would otherwise ensue; he confuses law and morality in a manner which has never been excelled before or since. If the philosophy of law is really so difficult and complicated a matter as Austin represents it, it is not worth studying; he makes a definition of law and then coolly informs us that all special acts of the legislature are not laws, since they do not agree with his definition. As an example, he states, on page 96, "An order issued by Parliament, stopping the exportation of corn then shipped would not be a law or rule, though issued by the sovereign legislature."

In fact, his whole book, in spite of his admirable ingenuity, may be considered a melancholy monument to the sad condition of our law, caused by the utter confusion of legal terms and ideas and our inability to form any system without an understanding of the history of these terms and ideas and their derivation from Roman and Germanic sources. That Austin himself regarded his book as a failure is shown by the fact that he always refused to undertake to arrange it for a new edition. His epitaph should be: "Magna conatus periit."

The great reputation and incomprehensibleness of Austin seems to have prevented other English writers from venturing upon the field of the theory of jurisprudence until within the last ten years. The authors of legal works were content to start with the terms law, right, sovereignty, etc., without offering any theory as to their origin. Recently, however, these questions are again being considered. Thus Sheldon Amos, Professor of Jurisprudence at the University College, London, has written some interesting books on codification and the science of law, but like Austin he is hopelessly befogged by the various meanings of legal terms and by lack of historical knowledge of jurisprudence. Thus, in his Science of Jurisprudence (vol. I, p. 1) he defines law as a command published by a sovereign political authority, but in the next page he says: "Law and government are born together, grow together and die together." It is difficult to understand how government can be the author of law and yet be born at the same time. In general he may be said to follow Austin in his definitions of law, sovereignty, etc., and the same disheartening lack of perspicuity characterizes his works. He considers that Bentham constructed the science of law and that Austin deserves the credit of its "conscious establishment" (Science of Law, p. 8). The works of the English theoretical writers would be far more valuable if they were less possitive in their tone and recognized the fact that no science of law exists at present, or is at present possible; that we are hopelessly befogged and our only salvation is in a careful, modest study of the historical development of our law, so as to clear away the errors and uncertainties which at present trip us up at every attempted advance. It is not well to cry: " Peace, peace, when there is no peace," or to build houses upon foundations of sand.

I will only refer to one other jurist who treats of the theory of law and its origin, namely, Mr. Willard, in his book on the " Law of Personal Rights," published by Appleton & Co., 1882.

He adopts the theory of the social contract as a necessary hypothesis. The following selections convey his views: " To find the origin of the principles and the rules of the law it is not necessary that resort should be had to actual historical facts" (p. 25). " We are to consider law as the expanded form of an obligation of a general nature" (p. 44). "According to legal ideas and for legal purposes the delegation of sovereign authority by the members of a society, to be exercised by the major part of such society, is absolute" (p. 29). " Upon the principles of legal construction the original intention of society must be regarded as creating sovereign power and lodging it for exercise in the hands of the majority of the community" (p. 27). We see, therefore, that he draws from the myth of an original contract, according to " legal ideas and for legal purposes," the very material result that majorities have absolute power in all communities. This is only another instance of how any form of government can be justified, if we only grant the hypothesis of an original contract. Hobbes proved the exclusive propriety of absolutism; Rousseau did the same for communism; Schoppenhauer derived constitutional monarchy, and Willard democracy, from the same source.

I will only add, concerning Mr. Willard's book, that its clearest parts are considerably more obscure than Mr. Austin's most involved ratiocinations.

If we turn from these English theoretical jurists to the English writers on the history of law, we find a wonderful difference. The latter, adopting the methods of the Savigny school, are producing even more important results from their acquaintance with the old laws of India and Ireland, which, as products of related Aryan races, are so useful in elucidating English and Roman law. Moreover, from the fact that England is the only modern Aryan race which has developed a legal system at all comparable to that of Rome, English lawyers can get a better idea of the actual substance of Roman law from the scattered decisions in the Corpus juris of Justinian than Continental jurists, whose natural law was stamped out centuries ago by attempted imitations of the Corpus juris.

As to theories of the origin of law, Phillimore contents himself with adopting the social contract theory as a necessary or useful hypothesis, and Maine states in his "Early History of Institutions" (p. 354): "The analysis of government and society and the determination of sovereignty are so nearly completed (by Hobbes) that little could be added to them by Bentham and Austin." As Savigny and his followers in Germany were frightened from investigations of legal philosophy by the high-sounding obscurity of Hegel, and contented themselves generally with adopting it blindly, so the English historical jurists were content to worship the vail behind which Bentham and Austin and their followers hid themselves.

Not so did Franz Lieber. His work is particularly valuable as a proof of what advantages residents of America have in the consideration of legal-political topics if they possess adequate theoretical knowledge, from the fact that they live in a land where the origin and growth of Germanic communities and States is under their immediate observation, and also from the fact that they are free from the preconceptions necessarily entertained by men whose salaries are paid by a monarchial government, and who have been brought up from their youth with ideas of and traditions in favor of certain forms of government.

The great importance of his work, in my opinion, lies in the fact that he expounded scientifically the Germanic theory known as self-government, as distinguished from the theories of absolute sovereignty. In his "Political Ethics" (volume I., page 352), he says that all states are autarchies or hamarchies (the latter word being derived from the Greek words signifying "jointly," and to rule). Autarchy is absolutism, or absolute power; hamarchy has an organic life, with distinct parts, with independent action, like an animal body; the form may be monarchy (as in England), or democracy (as in the United States). France, under Napoleon III., was an autarchy, with centralized, absolute government.

In his subsequent work on Civil Liberty, he develops this idea, terming it "institutional self-government," which he describes as "of an interguaranteeing and consequently interlimiting character, and in this aspect the negation of absolutism" (p. 319), and as requiring "that everything which can without general inconvenience be left to the circle to which it belongs, be thus left to its own management" (p. 321). This was the opposite to Rousseau's "inarticulated, unorganized, uninstitutional majority" (p. 372). Lieber therefore in my opinion, although he partly availed himself of the conclusions of Hegel, deserves the credit of being the first who met this social contract theory successfully, and gave a foundation of fact instead of fiction for our theories on law and government; although De Tocqueville, in his laudation of New England townships in his Democracy in America, had partly shown the way.

Had Lieber's Political Ethics been written but a few years earlier, so that Webster could have used it, as an arsenal, in his fight with Calhoun on nullification, the history of the United States might have been very different; as it is, however, I believe that our whole people owe him a large debt of gratitude. Mohl and other modern German writers of the so-called Professorial Socialist School have followed in and developed the same general line of thought, although they give too much authority and initiative to the State, instead of to the organizations between the State and the individual; they would force a growth from above, instead of awaiting a development from below.

Oliver Wendell Holmes, Jr., in his recent book on the Common Law, is another American writer who has steered clear of these Old World fogbanks, but he confines himself more particularly to questions of private law and the elucidation of the many historical problems, which must precede any successful attempt at construction of new law on our part; he makes the basis of law, however, too narrow, when he cites with approval Sir James Stephens' opinion, that its object is the gratification of revenge.

His whole book is a sign of great promise and indicates that we will have a race of American writers on political and legal topics, which will surpass that of any previous age or country, if we will only begin from the beginning and get rid of this conglomeration of Roman and Germanic theories and terminology.

III.

The most important role, however, which this theory of the social contract has played in the world's history, up to the present time, was in this country. It is true that the name appears comparatively seldom, and that its European authors are not often cited, for a very good reason, which will be later explained; but the fact remains, that had it not been for the influence of this theory, the history of the United States would have been very different. The men who guided the country through the Revolution and who afterwards formed the United States Constitution, were not perceptibly influenced by this theory; in neither the Articles of Confederation nor in the Constitution do the familiar terms of the supporters of the theory, such as "compact," "natural rights," "sovereignty," etc., appear, nor are they often used in the early State Constitutions, nor in the debates in the different State conventions on the adoption of the United States Constitution.

It is true that the Declaration of Independence is full of its "glittering generalities"; but it was the work of Jefferson, and was moreover, in my opinion, not considered of the same importance at that time, as at present. The people of all the different States, in the first place, had not authorized their delegates to sign it; the act of these delegates was therefore void. Secondly, many of the delegates did not sign until long after the date of the instrument, and some not at all. Thirdly, the States adopted separate declarations of independence in their State conventions—which were clearly not considered superfluous. Thus, the delegates of New York State were not authorized to sign the Declaration of Independence; they were also absent from Congress at that time and attending the State Constitutional Convention, which they apparently considered of more importance. The New York State Constitution, recites the Declaration of Independence, that after "most serious consideration," on July 9th, 1777, they had unanimously resolved that the reasons assigned therein are "cogent and conclusive." "This convention, therefore, in the name and by the authority of the good people of this State doth ordain, determine and declare that no authority shall on any pretense whatever be exercised over the people or members of this State, but such as shall be derived from or granted by them."

This statement shows how New York considered the Declaration; its simple, manly language is also in striking contrast to that of the Declaration, and is only one example of how little that line of thought was at that time appreciated in this country. In fact any one who will read the speeches and writings of that time will find but few traces of the influence of the social contract theory. The "Fathers" went straight ahead; they knew what they wanted, and they formed a typical Germanic State, consisting of ever larger associations of people, each association with powers to preserve the interests of its members, all united in one harmonious whole. The address of the representatives of New York to the citizens of the State, inciting them to resist Great Britain, is full of references to the Bible and the resistance of the chosen people to the tyrants, but contains no reference to the inalienable rights of man and other catch words of the social contract school.

When then did the social contract theory make its appearance? It was Jefferson who brought it back with him from Paris, where he had been during the formation of the Constitution, and presented, as his gift to the new-born country, the

Kentucky and Virginia resolutions of 1789—like the fairy god-mother who was not invited to the christening, and gave the spiteful wish which condemned the sleeping beauty to her hundred years sleep. Only in this case, the fatal gift was accompanied by no warning; the poison secretly worked its way into our country's system; the doctors knew not what the evil was and hence could not prescribe for it; four years of bloody war was the drastic remedy at last applied, and it is doubtful if we are yet free from its effects.

In these resolutions we have the theory full grown; that of Virginia declared that the powers of the Federal Government resulted from the compact to which the States are parties; that of Kentucky further declared that "as in all other cases of compact, among parties having no common judge, each party has an equal right to judge for itself, as well of infractions as of the mode and measure of redress."

I know that the Virginia resolution was introduced by Madison, and that in his report in the House of Delegates, (session 1799-1780) on the Virginia resolutions, he reiterated its assertions as "unexceptionably true in its several positions, as well as constitutional and conclusive in its inferences."

But the language and the ideas are so different from those of the Madison who worked so hard for the Constitution in the Convention and in the *Federalist*, that they must be ascribed to the influence of Jefferson, even if the latter had not acknowledged that he consulted with Madison about it.

Thus in the Virginia Convention in 1788 (Vol. III. of Elliott's Debates, p. 532,) Madison contradicts this resolution flatly: "It may be a misfortune that in organizing any government, the explication of its authority should be left to any of its co-ordinate branches. . . . With respect to the laws of the Union, it is so necessary and expedient that the judicial power should correspond with the legislative, that it has not been objected to."

The extent to which Jefferson influenced Madison in regard to this social contract theory, and the extent to which he was himself its victim, is shown by a letter from Paris, in which he in perfect good faith carries out Rousseau's theories to their natural consequences. He proposes what he declares to be the novel question of how one generation can bind another; as no way suggests itself to him, he concludes that it is impossible; therefore, since according to Buffon each generation lasts 19 years, at the end of that time all constitutions, laws and national contracts are void, and revolution and bankruptcy are necessary and legitimate. He suggests to Madison that he bring forward this theory publicly. Madison replied that he found it not "entirely compatible with the course of human events," and declined the honor, although he did not deny the correctness of the theory.

As is well known, Calhoun, when he proclaimed the doctrine of nullification, did not go beyond the words of these resolutions, and the Rebellion was only applying them practically.

Jefferson alone, however, could not have introduced this fatal theory, had the general opinion of educated men not at that time been so attracted by it, all over the civilized world, and it was nourished here by the Franco mania, which so long held sway over our society, and by the subsequent desire of the South to evade the true meaning of the Constitution.

So far as suited their purposes, the Southerners adopted Rousseau's theory completely, only they substituted the States for individuals, and claimed for them the same right to judge whether the terms of the compact, which they had formed, had been violated, and if the States decided that it had been violated, they had the same right to refuse to recognize the assumption of power and to declare the compact ended; this, as Calhoun claimed, was perfectly legal and was no rebellion; on the same theory, Rousseau's disciples had decapitated Louis XVI.

The opponents of nullification had unfortunately no theory to oppose to this social compact theory. The hatred of England, which followed the war of 1812, prevented the writings of Burke from gaining much credit; the later State constitutions and the decisions of the courts show how generally the social compact was accepted, and accepting this theory, the advocates of the Constitution were beaten, as a foregone conclusion.

This appears, for example, in the great debate between Calhoun and Webster on nullification. Calhoun's resolutions were a somewhat elaborate reiteration of the Virginia and Kentucky resolutions of the right of nullification, with the additional assertion that the people of these United States are not and have never been united on the principle of the social compact and formed into one nation or people.

Webster did not deny that this was the only principle on which governments could be formed; hence, of course, he could not prove that the United States were a nation; he relied in part on Hobbes' theory of the fearful consequences of dissolution of government, and in part on Kant's and Grotius' theories that the compact having been made, something unalterable had resulted therefrom. He says: "So the Constitution of the United States founded in or on the consent of the people, may be said to rest on compact or consent; but it is itself not the compact but its result. When a people agree to erect a government and actually erect it, the thing is done and the agreement is at an end."

Calhoun, in his reply, disposed of these assertions as

easily as Rousseau did of those of Grotius and Kant; he said: "I would ask to what compact does the Senator refer as that on which the Constitution rests? What can it be but that the Constitution is itself a compact? And how will his language read, when fairly interpreted, but that the Constitution was a compact, but is no longer a compact? It had by some means or another, changed its nature or become defunct."

Calhoun was therefore logically correct. If the governments can only be formed by compact, the United States government was plainly not formed by compact of the individuals (because they had voted to adopt it, only as members of the different States), hence the United States government could be formed only by the compact of the States; and, if so formed, each State had the right to construe the compact or declare it at an end.

The doctrine of absolute sovereignty, which always results from the social compact theory, was also imported to add weight to these conclusions. It was a necessary consequence upon which all writers, Grotius and Kant, as well as Hobbes and Rousseau, agreed that there must be absolute sovereignty somewhere; they derived this idea from the Greeks and Romans, and the only question was as to who should wield it. Calhoun in his article on the United States Constitution, says, on page 189: "Its (the revolution's) first and necessary effect was to cut the cord which had bound the colonies to the parent country—to extinguish all the authority of the latter—and by consequence to convert them into thirteen independent and sovereign States." And in his above cited speech on nullification, he says: "The whole sovereignty is in the several States, while the exercise of sovereign power is divided—a *part* being exercised under compact, through the general government, and the *residue* through the separate State governments." It is true that Calhoun knew of the true nature of a Germanic State, with its limited government, as he cites Palgrave to that effect; but he applied this necessity of limitation only to United States government, and considered the States as sovereign.

The theory was carried out practically when the constitutional conventions of the Southern States forced their States, often by small majorities, into the Rebellion. As Yancey said, in the Alabama convention of 1861: "But in this body is all power, no powers are reserved from it. The people are here in the persons of their deputies. Life, liberty and property are in our hands. All our acts are sumpreme without ratification, because they are the acts of the people acting in their sovereign capacity." Rousseau might have said that.

The reason why Rousseau was so seldom quoted was that he had followed out his principles to their natural consequences, which included the abolition of slavery. When arguing on this point, Calhoun adopted the strongest language of Grotius and Kant. For example, in his Disquisition on Government, he says: "Men are born in the social and political state; and of course, instead of being born free and equal, are born subject, not only to parental authority, but to the laws and institutions of the country where born, and under whose protection they draw their first breath." For a similar reason, the Northern men did not cite Rousseau's writings so often in their conflict against slavery, because they seemed to uphold so strongly the States' rights doctrine.

The upholders of the Union made here again the fatal mistake of recognizing the necessity of absolute sovereignty; if it exists, the United States has it not, nor have the people it, since it is an absurdity to talk of absolute sovereignty over oneself—the States certainly have the best claim to it. This admission is a mistake, which has lately been encouraged by the influence of Austin and

Bentham, who derived the idea from Hobbes. J. C. Hurd in his Theory of Our National Existence, and most of the judges of the Supreme Court, since the war, vainly labor to justify the acts of the North, by proving in some way the existence of sovereignty of the United States government, or of the people.

It cannot be done, because the Constitution and the men who framed it would have none of it; they formed a simple natural Germanic State, wherein the individuals grouped themselves into associations of different sizes, and endowed each association with the powers necessary to protect the interests, for whose protection that association was formed; and this system they did not intend, and would not allow to be broken up, by any of its members, who had entered it and accepted its benefits.

The idea of "sovereignty of the Nation" is as hostile to the real spirit of our institutions as was that of "sovereignty of the State;" both are equally un-Germanic and un-American. The worship of Nationality was developed by Napoleon I. to hide his overthrow of the Republic.

Our trouble has been that after our natural government was formed, the attempt was made to explain it by the terms of the social contract theory and to import into it ideas derived from the absolute governments of Rome and Greece, with the consequent ignoring of all constitutional rights.

What we need is to carry out the spirit of our Constitution. We are no longer merely an agricultural people, divided as to our interests, chiefly by geographical position, into towns, counties and States, but large cities have come into being, where men know each other, not as residents of the same ward, or district, but as members of the same trade, business or profession; these associations, with different common interests, should be recognized politically, and receive a proper share of the powers and duties of government, so that they may provide for and protect their interests.

That would be carrying out the federal spirit of our Constitution, and would secure us as long a lease of prosperity as we might have enjoyed under our present Constitution, intended for agricultural communities, had its real meaning not been perverted by the introduction of the social contract theory, that blight of our modern political development.

IV.

Let us now consider briefly the influence of this theory on the principal writers of political economy.

The idea of an absolute government, fostered by the social contract theory, produced the mercantile system, in which government considered it as its duty to regulate all industries of the country. Adam Smith led the reaction against this paternal government plan; in his Wealth of Nations he says: "All systems either of preference or of restraint being thus completely taken away the obvious and simple system of natural liberty establishes itself of its own accord. Every man is left perfectly free to pursue his own interest his own way. . . According to the system of natural liberty the sovereign has only three duties to perform: 1st. To ward off foreign invasion. 2d. To administer justice. 3d. To erect public works, which it would not be for the interest of a small number of individuals to erect." (Book V., Ch. 9.)

This system of "natural liberty," or *laissez-faire* as it was afterward called, was the natural result of Grotius' deification of the human reason. If that was sufficient to originate governments it must also be sufficient to discover the best and only right manner of conducting private business enterprises; and, as the right to govern depends theoretically upon the consent of the individual, and as this consent is so difficult to prove, the right must be exerted as rarely as possible.

It was seen that the State interfered too much with the individual upon the Continent, hence this school flew to the opposite extreme, that the "enlightened reason" of the individual must be considered as all-sufficient. It was applying the same reasoning to the business of individuals which Rousseau had applied to public affairs.

These ideas are not all acknowledged by Adam Smith, but they are evidently the motives which led to the adoption of his theory, and they are plainly declared by his followers. Thus, Bentham says in his "Principles of Legislation" (I., p. 32): "Every one makes himself the judge of his own utility; such is the fact, and such it ought to be; otherwise man would not be a rational agent."

And John Stuart Mill, in his "Political Economy," in his second volume, p. 515, says: "Unless the conscience of the individual goes freely with the legal restraint it partakes either in great or in small degree of the degradation of slavery. Scarcely any degree of utility, short of absolute necessity, will justify a prohibitory regulation, unless it can be made to recommend itself to the general conscience." . . . "*Laissez-faire* should be the general practice" (p. 524). Mill distinctly adopts the social contract theory as a necessary hypothesis. In his first volume (p. 244) he says: "In considering the institution of property we may suppose a community unhampered (?) by any previous possession . . . . bringing nothing with them but what belonged in common, and having a clear field for the adoption of the institutions and polity which they judged most expedient." Of course, Mill, no more than any of the other writers, can point to a time or place when this occurred; his whole argument has, therefore, the same value as those of the astronomers before Kepler's time, who based their conclusions upon various ingenious hypotheses, but not upon facts.

Mr. Mill illogically considers the rights of property-owners of things personal to be absolute and inviolable, but he applies Proudhon's arguments to the ownership of land, and demands the confiscation of the "unearned increment."

Mr. Mill is naturally opposed to trades-unions; thus he says in Book II., Ch. XIV., §6, of his Political Economy: "The time, however, is past when the friends of human improvement can look with complacency on the attempts of small sections of the community, whether belonging to the laboring or any other class, to organize a separate class interest in antagonism to the general body of laborers." In his celebrated theory that wages are regulated by the law of supply and demand, he passes by the unions as an unimportant factor. For this he was taken to task by W. T. Thornton in his book "On Labor" (London, 1869), who says: "Enough, it is hoped, has now been said to justify the further assertion that, in the actual condition of the world, unionism is to the employed in a double sense a necessity. It is indispensable alike for their protection and for their advancement" (p. 300).

Mr. Thornton, however, did not free himself from the prejudices of this English school against trades-unions; thus he says on p. 335: "Still, even when so modified and chastened, the necessity for its continuing to exist at all will continue to be an evil." The reason for this opinion is found in that Mr. Thornton, although he describes so eloquently the hardships of a workingman's life, fails to see that there is any question of justice in the relations between employers and employees. He says on p. 122; "Employers can equally, without injustice, accept the services of laborers on the very lowest terms to which the latter can voluntarily and with their eyes open be brought to submit. Neither party possesses any relative rights in the business except those which arise out of their mutual agreement or contract. Whatever else that contract may be, it cannot be iniquitous." Mr. Thornton very logically expects no consideration, on the other hand, from the trades-unions should they come into power, and consequently does not object to having them called a necessary evil. Mr. Mill, in an article in the *Fortnightly Review* for May, 1869, was forced to acknowledge in effect the pertinency of Mr. Thornton's criticism, and quotes with evident approval many of the latter's remarks concerning the benefits to be derived from trades-unions, although he does not in terms retract his theory of supply and demand as being the proper rule to govern the contracts between employers and employees.

Professor Cairnes, in his Political Economy (1874), practically reasserted Mr. Mill's heartless theory. He says on p. 263: "I am unaware of any rule of justice applicable to the problem of distributing the produce of industry; and, secondly, that any attempt to give effect to what are considered the dictates of justice which should involve as a means towards that end a disturbance of the fundamental assumptions on which economic reasoning is based—more especially those of the right of private property and the freedom of individual industry—would, in my opinion, putting all other than material considerations aside, be inevitably followed by the destruction or indefinite curtailment of the fund itself from which the remuneration of all classes is derived."

I will only refer to one other thorough-going supporter of the *laissez-faire* system—Professor Sumner of Yale—

who cannot fail to be an interesting figure as probably one of the last of his race. In his last book, "What Social Classes Owe to Each Other," he says: "In our modern state, and in the United States more than anywhere else, the social structure is based on contract; status is of the least importance. Contract, however, is rational—even rationalistic. In a state based on contract sentiment is out of place in any public or common affairs (p. 25). . . . It follows, however, that one man in a free state cannot claim help from and cannot be charged to give help to another (p. 27). . . . The relations of sympathy and sentiment are essentially limited to two persons only, and they cannot be made a basis for the relations of groups of persons or for discussion by any third party (p. 160). . . . There is no injunction, no 'ought' in political economy at all" (p. 156).

The great fault of this school lies in its undue exaltation of the individual, which followed as a natural reaction against the undue exaltation of the State; but this is as un-Germanic, as unsuited to the wants of our people as the former extreme. The present natural organization of a Germanic people is in many corporations, from the guild or trade-union up to the State, each of these having limited, independent duties to perform, corresponding to the interests which the members of each corporation have in common; among these corporations the State is the highest and last, but by no means the omnipotent or sole union.

The Germanic system of many organizations intermediate between the State and the individual, is referred to by Tacitus, as a characteristic of the primitive Germans in their native forests. It was by means of these comitatus that the enervated and depraved provinces of the Roman empire were conquered and divided into towns and counties; it was by means of these agricultural unions, which subsequently grew into the feudal system, that Europe was preserved during the middle ages from destruction by the ferocious Norsemen and the victorious Arabs; it was by means of similar unions or guilds when great cities began to spring up that these grew up and were able to defend themselves against their many enemies. And it was the destruction of the system in England under Henry VIII., which made the introduction of the Roman theory of an absolute government possible. How great a part these guilds played in European history is only now being recognized; Toulmin Smith's collection of charters shows how much of the work of our civilization was done through these organizations.

The principal evil effect of this social contract theory was, as above stated, that it left no place for these intermediate associations, but considered only the powerless individual and the almighty State, and up to the time of Rousseau delivered the former helplessly into the hands of the latter, although it recognized that, like Frankenstein's monster, the individual had produced this almighty State.

The reaction of the Manchester school in private affairs, and of Rousseau's school in public affairs, has made this mistake; it has gone too far; it denies the power of the State, but supplies no other form of union for individuals to follow out their common interests. Mill says: "The unit of society is not the family or clan . . . . but the individual" (vol. I., p. 262). Thus Bentham says in his Principles of Legislation (I., 83): " As a general rule the greatest possible latitude should be left to individuals, in all cases in which they can injure none but themselves—for they are the best judges of their own interests." The effects of this policy are more unfortunate in heterogeneous nations (if I may so name nations composed of various races) like the French, than in more homogeneous nations like the English or German because where a nation is composed of men of one stock, the theory of their equality is practically nearer the truth. But it is a crime and a wicked deed to tell men they are equal, when the doctrines of heredity show that different races of men have different capacities, which to a great measure necessarily fix their mode of life. To tell such different men that they are equal, is like telling a man who never was in deep water, to plunge off a dock without a life preserver, because, being a man, he must be equal to yonder expert swimmer.

From my reference to the difference of races of men and the doctrine of heredity, I would not have it inferred that I in any way adopt Herbert Spencer's theory that man is but a higher gregarious animal. His whole theory rests on the assumption that the Darwinian theory is proved; but I do not see how any man, certainly no lawyer, accustomed to distinguish assertions from evidence, can read the books of this school carefully without coming to the conclusion that they fail to make out a case; that there is not a missing link, but that every other link is missing, so that there is not the vestige of a chain. This absence of evidence is explained in various ways— that it perished millions of years ago or exists in the centre of Africa or Asia; but these explanations are not sufficient to take the place of the evidence and prove their case. If Herbert Spencer's theory were correct, it is then of no possible interest to us how the State is formed, any more than it is to the particles of matter which are about to be formed into a crystal, to which he compares the State. If the survival of the fittest is the law by which men are governed, then let us all take to ourselves the advice of the old man in Horace: "Make money; honestly, if you can—but make money!"

Spencer's political works remind me of the man who was going to make a great jump; but he went back so far to get a start, that he ran over a hill before he jumped. Spencer, in my humble opinion, is just starting up the hill. He tries to explain the action of men by the study of the roots of a potato plant; he says in his Data of Ethics (p. 96): "Here might be urged the necessity for preluding the study of moral science by the study of biological science." At all events, we can safely leave this "triangulation of the universe," this philosophy of the future, to the future.

No country is so heterogeneous as the United States, although the great majority belong to different families of the Germanic race; in no country has the system of individualism been carried to such an extent; in no country has the doctrine of equality been more productive of inequality, considering the brief time of the development of our industries. To tell you or me that we are on an equality with Vanderbilt before the law, is telling us what we know to be untrue.

Before the tariff, which the war necessitated, we were chiefly an agricultural community; the division according to our abodes into towns, counties and states, was proper and Germanic. Since, then, large cities have grown up, with the balance of power in the hands of great working populations, we should follow the Germanic precedent, set to us in the 13th, 14th and 15th centuries, and have these workingmen, and business men and all professions organized to look after their common interests. They will protect themselves; they will prevent tramps and loafers stealing the results of their labors; they will check the arrogance of our railroad barons far better than either the absolute State or the individual can do. This theory of limited sovereignty and unions intermediate between the individual and the State,

I believe to be the solution of the most pressing problem of the day, in political economy as well as in politics.

The late W. Stanley Jevons, in his "State in Relation to Labor" (1883), fully recognizes this necessity. He says on p. 6 of the introduction: "One result which clearly emerges from a calm review is that all classes of society are trades-unionists at heart, and differ chiefly in the boldness, ability and secrecy with which they push their respective interests."

But, like the other English economists, he looks back to the theory of co-operation (in spite of all its practical failures) as a desideratum for laborers; so that, although the book last cited contains much that is suggestive, the whole subject of the proper future development of these trade organizations and their place in the State remains a sealed book to the English economists, as well as to their great authorities on the history and theory of law and politics—dominated as they have been by the atheistic tendencies of Bentham and Mill.

From this brief statement of the positions of our principal authorities in law, politics, and political economy, who based their theories, tacitly or confessedly, directly on the social contract theory, and ultimately upon the belief in the arbitrary creation of law by man, we are justified in concluding that these theories practically lead, in politics, to the advocacy of absolute sovereignty and the destruction of the lesser organizations existing between the individual and the State, and the substitution of an absolute unconstitutional government of the masses or of an emperor. Moreover, in political economy we must see that these same theories lead either to communism or to the entire independence of the individual in business affairs from the dictates of morality, and the denial of the propriety of any organization placing a limit upon the degradation to which human beings may reduce themselves or others, and that in law they lead to reckless attempts to create the whole social fabric anew, by voluminous codes, and to insisting upon all principles of law being cast in the unbending form of statutes, no matter how many individual cases may be decided unjustly in consequence.

Meanwhile, the advocates of these theories are forced to confess that the present result of their propaganda has not been satisfactory, that the outlook is lowering, and that they have no remedy to offer, except maintaining the same course.

That the conclusions of this school are hostile to the spirit of the teachings of the Fathers who formed our Government, as indicated by the extracts from the *Federalist* at the head of this article, is apparent.

Is there any doctrine as to the origin of law which justifies these theories of Federalism, and have they any application to the present? In England, France and Germany the three great champions of what we have ventured to call Federalism were Burke, Montesquieu and Stahl. Burke, that great admirer of our American Federal Government, declared in his speech against Warren Hastings: " No man can lawfully govern himself according to his own will; much less can one person be governed by the will of another. We are all born in subjection, all born equally high and low, governors and governed in subjection to one great, immutable, pre-existent law, prior to all our devices, and prior to all our contrivances. This great law does not arise from our conventions and compacts; on the contrary, it gives to our conventions and compacts all the force and sanction they can have."

The same spirit was represented in France by Montesquieu, in the words: "Laws are the necessary relations which spring from the nature of things. . . . Before there were intelligent beings, these beings were possible; they had, therefore, relations and, consequently, possibly laws. . . . God made these laws because they have a relation to His wisdom and power."

In Germany, Stahl in his " Philosophy of Law (vol. II., p. 219), declared : " The prototype of law is God's plan of creation, as the ideal of the beautiful in the human form is the standard which guides the sculptor and in comparison with which his work is judged."

Federalism, in my opinion, must be based on the opinion that the spring of law lies, not in human reason or in human fear, but in the sympathy for our neighbor, which God has given us.

It is the teaching of Christianity in the parable of the unjust servant, of whom his fellow servants complained to their master for his harshness towards one of their number, and whom the master then punished so severely.

Do we not all feel that if we were placed in a position in which all our physical wants were satisfied, and yet saw one of our fellow-beings constantly maltreated that we would sacrifice some of our material comforts, in the first place, to relieve his sufferings, and then to punish the man who had inflicted these sufferings?

The true measure of civilization is the extent of this feeling of sympathy, and the great impulse to improvement in civilization is its development.

The mere statement of the penalty to be inflicted on the man who commits a certain act is not the whole law; that is only the prohibitory or negative side. Law consists in the will of a people that individuals should show, by their acts, that they have a certain amount of sympathy towards each other, in the various relations of life. Law is, therefore, positive and mandatory; it prescribes the rules which individuals should observe towards each other, in their relations of owner, employer, contractor, husband or wife, parent or child.

The only way to accomplish the object of law is to go further back than the legislature or the police courts, and develop in man that sympathy which will gradually make law unnecessary; as in medicine, the great aim of modern science is to keep men healthy, rather than to cure them by noxious doses, after the disease is incurred. The State cannot disregard the development of the ethical side of the character of its citizens—increase of sympathy decreases crime.

But man need not seek in theories, founding law upon what may have happened in pseudo-prehistoric times, for an excuse to justify his insisting upon the exercise of a certain amount of sympathy by his fellow-men towards each other, if he believes that this desire is given him by God, and intended to be the means by which he prepares himself and others for a future life. If a man loves not his brother, whom he has seen, how can he love God, whom he has not seen?

Our object here should be to realize the brotherhood of man. We can work for this by developing our sympathy for each other as individuals, or as members of our various trades or professions, or as members of the State.

Primitive man has this sympathy towards the members of his immediate family; tribes are formed by the extension of this sympathy to related families; the Germanic comitatus, the feudal system, the guilds of the middle ages are but products of this extended feeling of sympathy to individuals, with whom we are thrown together in common undertakings. By sympathy I mean here such as shows itself not in words but in deeds; people at different stages of their development have their power of sympathy necessarily differently developed; they cannot extend it at will to embrace further circles.

These organizations, intermediate between the individual and the State, have therefore objects to accomplish arising from love of neighbor as well as the individual or the State.

The great misfortune which the social contract theory brought with it, as I have already stated, was the abolition of the guilds and feudal and corporative ties, by which Germanic Europe was then bound together into smaller bodies, and the attempt to substitute for this sympathy the feeling of nationality, which the Greeks had developed for their small cities and which was not applicable to large, thinly peopled countries.

The Germanic race at that time was not able to send forth this sympathy. Rousseau and his followers called in vain for fraternity; they could possibly produce liberty and equality, but fraternity lay in the human will, and that they could not touch. But while they did not accomplish their object they managed to abolish instead of reforming the intermediate associations between the State and individual, within which the people at that time had sympathy.

This sympathy—from which springs this desire to avenge the injuries of others—is, therefore, the root of all organizations of men into guilds, corporations and States. It is the origin of all law; and, as it extends to wider circles, families, tribes, guilds, cities and States are organized.

The injuries to be avenged, and the extent of the vengeance, should depend upon the development of the feeling of sympathy in that particular people.

If the law does not correspond to and satisfy this want, people will satisfy the craving without resorting to law, in the same way as they would satisfy their physical wants of hunger and thirst. There is no essential difference between criminal law and civil law; the redress of the wrongs to which the latter apply is merely left to the initiative of the party injured. The crimes to be punished, and the penalties to be imposed, should, therefore, be considered as carefully, with reference to the particular wants of a people, as its food or water supply.

If punishments are too low, people will resort to Lynch law, or personal revenge. A large portion of crime, which our courts punish, is due to bad criminal and civil law.

And yet, to-day, no public indignation is visited upon our so-called representatives at Albany, when they, year after year, pass voluminous statutes, called codes, purporting to regulate the satisfaction of this most important want of our nature, without inquiry or discussion; although the greatest interest is taken by the public in a bill affecting our water supply, street cars, or other physical want.

As before stated, I believe that this indifference is largely due to the opinion that laws are purely human creations, originating from man's unaided reason, and which he may, with propriety, change at pleasure, in place of the belief that they should be in accord with eternal principles of justice, applicable to human relations, which it is man's highest privilege and duty to study, ascertain and apply.

It follows also in politics, that the whim of a temporary majority of a people is not infallible, but that the great principles which a race is seeking to realize should be placed permanently in well-guarded constitutions, and that men should yield absolute government over themselves, or sovereignty, to no individual or number of individuals, irrespective of these eternal principles of right and wrong.

It follows, also, in political economy, that we are not justified in permitting any system of business methods which steadily reduces its employees to conditions which prevent their physical and moral development, and their spiritual preparation for a life in the world to come ; and also that the existence and participation in government of organizations which prevent men from not only destroying themselves or others, but from making themselves or others physical or moral plague spots, is perfectly justified.

An unprejudiced and careful examination of the authors, above briefly referred to, can, as I believe, lead only to the conclusion that all theories are insufficient if they do not acknowledge that the fear of the Lord is the beginning of wisdom

In the words of Plutarch : " It is easier to build a city without foundations, than a State without a God."

In the words of Maurice : " The Apostles did not dare, they did not find it possible to think of human society, except as constituted in Christ. It was the confusion, the unbelief of men, to regard themselves as capable of fellowship and of existence without him. It was theirs to proclaim that there could be no families, no nations, to resist the selfish tendencies, which each of us is conscious in himself, and complains of in his neighbors, if there had not been one living centre of the whole body of humanity, one head of every man."

UNIVERSAL SUFFRAGE IN CITIES.

LAST spring, when the great Statue of Liberty arrived in this city, it was accepted,—as I judge from the speeches and editorials of that time,—as a symbol and reminder of the important military aid which the French monarchy rendered us during our struggle for independence. But I believe that there is also another boon which we owe to the French Republic, which is, in my opinion, at least equal to this military assistance. I refer to Universal Suffrage, which, while it has become so acclimated here, as to be generally considered *the* American political idea, still was in fact imported from France. What has been its reception?

The Federal party would have none of it. At the time of our Revolution, and at the time of the adoption of our Constitution, it was in force in none of the States. In this State of New York, an interest in real estate was required for all voters. This was abolished only after a hard struggle, in the convention of 1821, and against the energetic protest of such men as Chancellor Kent and Judge Spencer.

The change was due to the Democratic Party, following especially the great theories of Jefferson, who in turn drew his inspirations from the French philosophers of the 18th century, in opposition to the narrow, colonial ideas of the Federalists, who could imagine no better government than that of a British squirarchy, and whose leader, Hamilton, declared himself in favor of that government as a model, although it was "bottomed in corruption," and although he confessed that to strike out that corruption, would render it impracticable.

It was *Jefferson* who wrote to David Hartley :

"I have no fear but the result of our experiment will be that men may be trusted to govern themselves, without a master. Could the contrary of this be proved, I should conclude either that there was no God, or that he is a malevolent being."

And yet I cannot be surprised, if, what I have said, should call forth in this club half derisive smiles, such as the Roman augurs wore, in Cicero's time, when performing their mysterious rites, out of sight of the public. No set of men, perhaps, are better acquainted with the practical working of our government,—especially in this great city; we know how much it is a government "of the people, by the people, and for the people." We know about what it costs to get a nomination to the Legislature or the Bench ; we know what chance a measure for the general public good has on its merits in the Legislature or in the Board of Aldermen ; we know for what considerations the city is allowed to remain full of moral plague spots ; we know how often "reform" and "public spirit" have been the screen under whose cover public offices have been gained, only to be used for selfish ends.

And if we turn from our personal experience, and consult the writers in the magazines of the day, how few do we find of any importance, who have a good word to say for this universal suffrage! I will only cite a few passages. Thus the historian, Parkman, says in his article in the *North American Review* (vol. 127), entitled " Failure of Universal Suffrage : "

"More and more we drift into the condition of those unhappy -ountries where 'the post of honor is a private condition.'"

"What sort of statesmanship these forty millions produce, let the records of Congress show."

"Our politics do not invite, and hardly even admit, the higher and stronger faculties to a part in them."

"Liberal education is robbed of its best continuance and consummation, in so far as it is shut out from the noblest field of human effort, the direction of affairs of State."

"It is in the cities that the diseases of the body politic are gathered to a head, and it is here that the need of attacking them is most urgent. Our cities have become a prey."

Goldwin Smith, in *Putnam's Magazine* (vol. 43, p. 71), says:

"That Universal Suffrage, in the strict and literal sense of the term, has failed in some respects and produced serious evils, assuredly is not to be denied. While the wealthier classes have lost, the poorer have in no way gained by municipal pillage, which has enriched the demagogues alone. Witness the condition of the poorer quarters of New York."

And again Cuthbert Mills, in *International Review* of 1880, p. 209:

"Universal suffrage has broken down in cities."

Macaulay, writing to Henry S. Randall, says:

"It is quite plain that your government will never be able to restrain a distressed and discontented majority. There is nothing to stop you. Your constitution is all sail and no anchor. As I said before, when a society has entered on this downward progress, either civilization or liberty must perish. Thinking thus, of course, I cannot reckon Jefferson among the benefactors of mankind."

Other similar articles are "The Failure of Universal Suffrage," in *North American Review*, for July, 1878; Robert Lewes' article, "Mr. Gladstone on Manhood Suffrage," in 28*th Fortnightly Review*, p. 734; "Universal Suffrage in the United States, and its Consequences," in *Fraser's Magazine*, July, 1862.

But only one magazine article have I found in favor of this democratic doctrine, "Suffrage a Birthright," by Geo.

W. Julian, in *International Review*, for January, 1879, and even that writer admits the existence of grave evils under our present system,—only offers the stale denunciation of the recreancy of the better sort of men of all political parties.

And must we not all admit that the gravest evils do exist? That this country is not realizing the bright promises of its youth; that we consider ourselves happy to get rulers, who at least preserve a show of regard for the dictates of ordinary honesty?

And is it not so, that among the men we meet, it is becoming more and more usual to have them lay the blame for this state of things at the door of Universal Suffrage, and to hear the wish expressed that this right should be limited, in some way, either by a property or educational test?

But, Mr. President, I consider that it is worse than idle to talk of limiting universal suffrage; it has become inextricably woven into our theories and institutions.

Moreover, I do not think that, if they were practicable, either an educational or a property test would be desirable. As Mr. Julian said in the above cited article:

> "That a government basing its authority on the doctrine of inalienable rights, and professing to derive its powers from the consent of the governed, would continue to impose a property qualification upon voters, was a manifest political absurdity."

Or as Benjamin Franklin puts it:

> "Suppose a man owns a jackass worth $100, and that property confers upon him the right to vote: very well, he votes, but in the next year the death of the animal deprives the man of the vote; was it then the man, or the jackass who voted?"

Every inhabitant of a country pays taxes directly or indirectly, and suffers from their increase; every man is liable to be drafted for the common defence; every trade or business can be ruined by the ordinances of the Board of

Aldermen, or laws of the Legislature. What concerns all must be approved by all. To exclude one class works evil both on the governing and on the governed. The latter lose interest in public affairs and become a dangerous element; the former assume that everything must yield to their class interest, and the history of oligarchies shows only an invariable increase of class pride and arrogance.

Moreover, no one who is accustomed to mingle with rich and poor can say that one class or the other has a monopoly of the vices or of the virtues.

An educational test would afford no criterion of the moral qualities of the voter, for, as Herbert Spencer has shown, education cannot touch that will, which guides a man's actions and which lies back of his intellect. As Seneca says: "*Velle non discitur.*" Besides men of the student class acquire or lose something which unfits them —as we all know—to a certain extent from practical business affairs; and, if this is so, in the small affairs of daily life, still more manifest would it become in public affairs,— as is also shown by history.

If then neither an educational nor a property qualification of the suffrage is practicable or desirable, what is the cause of these present evils? I believe a glance at the constitutional history of our State will show why universal suffrage in our cities has produced such poor public officials and legislators.

The Constitution of 1777 provided for the election of 24 Senators from four great districts, and 70 Assemblymen, divided among the different counties. The Constitution of 1821 directed that 32 Senators be chosen from 8 districts, and 128 Assemblymen from different counties. The result was that several Senators and several Assemblymen were voted for by the inhabitants of one county or city, on a general ticket.

The Constitution of 1846 changed this by requiring one Senator to be elected from each of the 32 senatorial districts, and by directing the Board of Supervisors of each county to divide that county into districts, containing an equal number of inhabitants, which districts were each to elect one Assemblyman. In the discussions in the Legislature, which led to calling this convention, this innovation had not been considered. This change was not effected without strong opposition; 12 of the 15 New York representatives, including such men as Charles O'Connor, David R. Floyd-Jones and Samuel J. Tilden, voted against it. Mr. Chatfield said:

> "But the more serious objections were that you would get up 59 gerrymandering bodies, to cut up counties with reference rather to party objects than anything else. A county is an identity, an individual, so far as its interests were represented on this floor. Why then seek to distract this identity of interests, by breaking up its representation on this floor? The effect of this representation coming here divided, would be to cause the interests of the county to suffer, as each man would hold himself responsible only to the constituency of his district. It would make mince-meat of the counties for mere political ends."

Mr. Tilden denied that the sentiment of the people of New York had been expressed in favor of any districts.

Mr. Kennedy hoped:

> "That the Convention, before it adjourned, would see the injustice done to the City of New York, by obliging a division of it into four separate districts."

None of New York's representatives spoke in favor of the change; the only arguments for it came from county members in the large senatorial districts, who "wanted to know their Senator, to shake hands with him."

What has been the effect of this change in our cities? From that time dates the political decline of the Legislature of the State of New York. Mr. Marcy was not returned to the U. S. Senate, and if we except William H. Seward, who was the leading spirit of this Convention of 1846, that position has since then seldom, if ever, been filled by a statesman such as should represent the Empire State, and ably play a part in the history of the country, proportionate to the importance of our State. From that time dates the decline of our primaries in New York City ; prior to 1846, business men made a practice of attending primaries, and enjoyed the feeling that they were taking part in the government of the country. But by 1850, primaries had become what we see them to-day.

The discussions in the Legislature, which prior to that time were so full of wit and wisdom, degenerated, and members spent their energies chiefly in efforts to secure places and shower favors on the men who ran these primaries. Our city representatives allow millions every year to be raised by taxation in this City of New York, and to be distributed among the agricultural counties of the State. The real interests of our city are not represented. When a great body like the Produce Exchange, or the Stock Exchange, or the Bar Association, or the County Medical Society, sends representatives to Albany, to avert some threatened evil, little or no assistance can they get from the city's representatives ; in fact, as a rule, they find that the men from New York in the Legislature, are their worst foes, and the only assistance they can get is from representatives of the rural districts.

These latter frequently ask half contemptuously, why we do not send better representatives, and complain that the whole State is injured by their ignorance and venality. And yet the men of New York City show no decline in the sagacity of their management of private affairs.

Our business men still hold the commerce of this continent in their grasp ; the city is rapidly becoming the centre of art and literature, and especially all questions relating to political economy and government, receive great attention. Why do our legislators so unworthily represent all this accumulation of practical and theoretical knowledge and ability? It is in vain to adjure the so-called better classes to attend primaries ; the reception of the last resolution to that effect, offered in this club, showed how little faith we had in any such appeal. The great mass of citizens will not come. Their acquaintances live scattered all over the city ; the men, with whom they have common interests, which may be furthered or injured by the Legislature, are the men whom they meet every day in their exchanges, courts, manufactories and shops. With the increase of rapid transit the tie of locality in our cities is becoming daily less ;—what interests, as such, has a man living on the East side of a Third Avenue distinct from those of a man living across the street, so that they must have different representatives, or what interest has he, which is at all likely to be affected by legislation, in common with the man who lives on the same side of the street, so that they must vote for the same Solon. The man whom he thinks best calculated to ward off in the Legislature some evil, which threatens to destroy his means of gaining a living in his business, trade or profession, very probably lives many blocks off, perhaps at the other end of the city; his fellow tradesmen or businessmen may live scattered throughout the 24 districts, so that it is impossible for them, ever, in any one district, to unite and elect a representative of their most important interests. On the other hand, an unimportant interest, whose members happen to live in the same neighborhood, sends a number of representatives, far larger than its importance demands. In fact, the geographical division of the inhabitants of cities, for the purpose of electing members of the Legislature, is a false and artificial one, which has no connection with the real organizations of the people ; a city should be a political unit. The great strides of our civilization date from the 13th and 14th centuries, when cities were recognized as political units.

The great reform in city government, produced by the Roosevelt bills, consisted in taking power from the Board of Aldermen, whose members are elected from geographical districts, and in giving that power to the Board of Estimate and Apportionment and the Mayor, who are elected on a general ticket.

Our system of electing representatives is copied from rural institutions, where the division of farmers into townships by geographical lines secures a division of the inhabitants, according to their most important interests, since the farmers of the same neighborhood depend, as a rule, on the same principal product of the soil. But in cities, where men do not live on the products of the soil, this same division secures the very opposite results, and prevents men from sending to the Legislature representatives of their strongest interests.

At present, religious and other associations, which embrace the whole city, are gaining an undue influence in politics.

How can this evil be ended? What must be done to give Universal Suffrage the position it should hold in the hearts of our people?

I believe the answer comes to us again from the home of Universal Suffrage—from France.

The *Assemblée Nationale* of 1789, declared that France should be divided into a number of large districts, and that each district should return a number of representatives in proportion to the number of its inhabitants. The second Republic of 1848, adopted the same principle of electing a number of representatives from a large district on a general ticket. The third Republic of 1870, did the same. And each time the enemies of the Republic succeeded in cheating the people out of this system, because the latter did not fully understand its importance, and in introducing the system of elections on a single ticket from small districts, and in each case the fall of the Republic was the expected result.

Gambetta in his speech in favor of election by general ticket, or *scrutin du liste*, on November 11, 1875, declared:

"I give the Empire credit for having understood the power of democracy to the point of wanting to trouble its source."

And a few days later, he said:

"The laws which regulate the manner of voting are as essential for the future of society, as even those laws which acknowledged and established the Republic.'

Can we not,—who know the character of our average city legislators, elected on the single ticket system,—imagine how it was possible for Napoleon III. to rule France, with a legislature elected on the principle of Universal Suffrage? And why, under this present Republic, all its enemies united to banish the *scrutin du liste* in 1875, and to resist every attempt of Gambetta to bring it back?

But while that true Republican did not live to see the triumph of this system, for the realization of which he strained his whole giant energies, yet it has come to pass at last; and this fall, France is to elect a legislature with *scrutin du liste*, or on a general ticket in large districts.*

In the words of our poet:

> "The thoughts great hearts once broke for,
> We breathe cheaply in the common air;
> The dust we trample heedlessly,
> Throbbed once in saints and heroes rare;
> Who perished,—opening for the race
> New pathways to the common place."

---

* The result of this election in returning an increased number of conservative delegates and defeating many ministerial deputies, shows how idle were the fears

Not only the French have recognized this principle of election by general ticket, as the foundation of Universal Suffrage, but probably the greatest of modern English political thinkers,—John Stuart Mill, in his "Considerations on Representative Government," thus expresses himself, (on page 167):

> "But I cannot see why the feelings and interests which arrange mankind according to localities should be the only ones thought worthy of being represented, or why people who have other feelings and interests, which they value more than they do their geographical ones, should be restricted to these as the sole principle of their political classification."

And Mr. Mill's whole laudation of the scheme of cumulative voting, invented by Mr. Hare, springs evidently from his dissatisfaction with the present system of representation of small geographical districts; as he says on page 157:

> "The member would represent persons, not the mere bricks and mortar of the town, the voters themselves, not a few vestrymen or parish notables."

Thomas Jefferson adopted this system of election by a general ticket, in his draft of a Constitution for Virginia.

Since then we see that this system of election of several legislators, on a general ticket, from a large district, like our City of New York, was introduced by the Fathers, who gave us our National and our first State Constitution, and remained in force for two generations, during which our State held its own in our political history, and its government was administered by the best men it produced, and since this system was subsequently abolished without good reason, without full discussion, and against the protest of

---

of those who predicted a victory of the communists, or absolute power to the professional politicians. Rochefort, instead of heading the ticket, is doubtful of his election.

such wise men as Charles O'Conner, David R. Floyd-Jones and Samuel J. Tilden, and since our brother Republicans in France have recognized this question of the manner of electing representatives to be of the very essence of Universal Suffrage, and since such great writers as Mill commend it theoretically, and since no other practical remedy to the apparent and ever increasing evils of our government is offered,—why should we not return to this plan of making the city a political unit, and electing representatives of the whole of it, and not of its dissected parts? Might we not thus secure again a representative government, worthy of the Empire State?

To make a beginning, should not the cities be represented in the State conventions as a whole, by electing their delegates on a general ticket? This is now in fact done, when Tammany Hall, Irving Hall and the County Democracy are each awarded representation, without reference to their numerical strength in the different districts, but in proportion to their influence in the city as a whole. Let it be announced that the 24 Democrats, receiving the largest number of votes from the whole city, are to be sent to the convention, and I believe that you will see the whole city take an interest in the primaries, and that you will see 24 men elected of whom the Democratic party and our city will be proud.

The problem cannot be solved by reference to authorities of the past, when a little over three per cent. of the population lived in cities of more than 8000 inhabitants, while now in this State more than 50 per cent. live in such cities. Our constitution was intended for an agricultural population, and the wonder is that it has sufficed at all with so few changes to suit our altered circumstances. The Democratic party cannot be content with the cry: "We have Jefferson for our father."

Jefferson wrote to Madison on December 20, 1787, from Paris:

> "This reliance cannot deceive us as long as we remain virtuous; and I think we shall be so as long as agriculture is our principal object, which will be the case while there remain vacant lands in any part of America. When we get piled upon one another in large cities, as in Europe, we shall become corrupt, as in Europe, and go to eating one another as they do here."

No part of the world holds so dense a population as that part of this city which is bounded on the north by 14th Street and on the west by Broadway. Strong measures are needed; our cities are the great centres upon whose welfare that of the country depends; the task before this generation is as important as and perhaps more difficult than that which confronted the writers of the Federalist.

The public affairs of our villages are, as a rule, not so well administered after they receive a city charter; I believe the reason to be that villages are generally governed by trustees, who are elected by the whole community, on a general ticket, instead of by a Board of Aldermen, each member of which is elected from a single district.

The Mayors of our cities are, as a rule, chosen from among our best citizens and are far superior to the Aldermen.

No lawyer doubts that better judges could be obtained for our district courts, if they were elected by the city at large; their inferiority in learning and character to the judges of our general city courts is far greater than any difference in salary would warrant.

If we can elect a respectable Mayor, President of the Board of Aldermen and half a dozen judges in one year, why can we not also elect a number of respectable legislators on a general ticket?

The innumerable amendments to the charter of the city, during the last fifty years, have been mostly caused by the necessity of taking one power after the other from the Board of Aldermen and of giving it to officials or boards elected on a general ticket, or appointed by an official elected on such a ticket.

This movement culminated in the Reform bills of 1884, which took the right of confirmation from the Board of Aldermen and gave the uncontrolled power of appointment to the Mayor.

These improvements came from the exertions of committees of 50, 70 or 100, selected from the city at large, without reference to the districts; why could not the control of our municipal affairs be always in the hands of a committee of such character?

The reckless manner in which the Board of Aldermen exercises its only remaining power, in giving away the public streets, shows that this too must shortly be taken from these "deestrick" representatives, and given to a Board elected on a general ticket, or placed under the control of the Board of Estimate and Apportionment.

The indirect benefits of these reform bills is already becoming apparent in the decreased influence of the Halls; like Flood Rock after the explosion, they are rent with fissures and honeycombed with chasms, and only the shell remains.

The next task for reform is to abolish the rest of these geographical election districts in cities and to elect our Assemblymen and Senators from the city at large. Let our citizens group themselves according to their most important interests and not according to the places, where they happen to sleep at night, and let those important interests send representatives to the Legislature, to meet those of our fellow-citizens who live by agriculture.

So long as we keep these *artificial* districts, they must be worked by *machines;* and the machine which uses the most "soap" will win. No party which tries to carry out the letter and spirit of civil service reform can now remain in power; civil service reformers must strike deeper and remove the cause for the demand for the political worker, otherwise their Civil-Service Commissioners will sooner or later be politicians, who will use this centralized power to the greater detriment of the country. Remove this demand for "workers," and the constitutional method of selecting public officials will suffice.

Men are bound to create associations to further their important interests and to seek to have them represented in the Legislature; if the Constitution does not provide for their natural recognition they will spring up and work outside of the law and become a danger to the State.

Our mistake has been in following too blindly the example of the Germanic township,—so lauded in its New England form by De Tocqueville,—but we have overlooked the essential difference between an agricultural community and an arbitrary aggregation of city blocks.

De Tocqueville says in his "Democracy in America" (p. 67):

> "It is important to remember that they (townships) have not been invested with privileges, but that they seem on the contrary, to have surrendered a portion of their independence to the state. ..... The New Englander is attached to his township, because it constitutes a strong and free social body of which he is a member, and whose government claims and deserves the exercise of his sagacity."

Does this apply to our geographical election districts in cities?

Can it apply to any geographical sub-division of our city?

There will be no devotion to the city's interests and no civic pride, and but little devotion to the State, so long as the city is not recognized as a member of the State and represented as such, and its citizens allowed to group themselves naturally and select their real representatives.

The evil influences of the bad government and bad representation of our cities cannot be over-estimated ; if they continue, our civilization may be endangered, especially by reckless attempts at codification. In fact, the less our Legislature does, beyond what is absolutely required for the necessities of the hour, the better ; the prevalence of this sentiment is shown by the general demand for biennial sessions. A constitutional convention will be held bef re long in this State ; according to precedent, several members will be elected on a general ticket from each Senatorial district, and a number of representatives from the State at large. In former years, these bodies were composed to a large degree of the ablest and most experienced men in the State. Could not our cities, from such a Convention, regain a system of true representation, and establish on firm Democratic principles, for ages to come, Universal Suffrage—the pedestal of our American Liberty ?

The following lists show the occupations of the candidates from the election districts, as given in the EVENING POST *of October 29th:*

ALDERMEN:

Liquor Dealers 19	Truckman 1
No business except politics 7	Poultry dealer 1
Lawyers 3	Shoemaker 1
Clerks 3	Undertaker 1
Stone-yard owners 2	Saddler 1
Stable keepers 2	Janitor 1
Oyster dealers 2	Cigar dealer 1
Jewellers 2	Casemaker 1
Butcher 1	Mechanic 1
Butter dealer 1	Publisher 1
Fish dealer 1	Real Estate broker 1
Provision dealer 1	Inspector in Custom House 1
Plumber 1	

SENATORS:

No business except politics 4	Undertaker 1
Lawyers 5	Butcher 1
Merchants 2	Real Estate 1
Lumber Dealer 1	

ASSEMBLYMEN:

No business except politics 14	Merchant 1
Clerks 13	Butcher 1
Lawyers 10	Baker 1
Liquor dealers 7	Mason 1
Business unknown 3	Provision Dealer 1
Truckmen 1	Ex-policeman 1
Auctioneer 1	Peddler 1
Fish dealer 1	Ice-cart driver 1
Milk dealer 1	Builder 1
Stable-keeper 1	Lumber dealer 1
Real estate 1	

Argument in Favor of Electing Aldermen on a General Ticket.

THE Spring Election and Aldermanic bill, providing among other things for the election of Aldermen on a general ticket from the City at large, with cumulative voting, deals confessedly with a difficult subject. From De Tocqueville to President Woolsey and Governor Seymour we have innumerable laudations of the rural township system; but, when the government of cities is reached, a few sentences of mournful lament over their wickedness suffice and, like the Levite in the parable, they pass by on the other side. And yet all confess that this problem of good city government is of the utmost importance for our future civilization.

The two points in this bill to which I wish to call particular attention are the practical advantages to be derived from the election of Aldermen on a general ticket from the City at large, and the question of the constitutionality of the provision for cumulative voting,—as I understand that the gentlemen representing the City Reform Club intend to state the reasons for the other changes contemplated by this bill.

The evils which this bill is intended to remedy are so well known, that it is needless for me to dwell upon them here; it is hardly possible that our Board of Aldermen can sink lower than it has done.—The Board of 1884 was not a particularly bad one,—so far as one could judge from general behaviour and appearance of its members;—it seemed to me to be somewhat an improvement on that of 1883, which was the first Board elected exclusively from districts.

The reason the Board of 1884 became so notorious was that it was in 1884 that the law was passed authorizing the Aldermen to grant franchises to City railroads; that Board was the first which had this opportunity.—No one who has had dealings with the Board of 1885 will claim that it was composed of a class of men superior to its predecessors. It was my fortune to have considerable to do with those three boards, in the capacity of counsel for the Citizens' West Side Association,—an organization which desired to lessen the evils caused by the running of steam cars through the streets on the west side of the City;—and I confess that in my opinion, the interests of the citizens at large received as much attention from one of these Boards as it did from the other.

The whole history of the innumerable changes of our charter is explained by the necessity of taking one by one all the powers from the Aldermen, and of giving them to officers elected from the City at large, or to their appointees.—This work was thought to be practically completed when the Committee of Fifty-three secured the passage of the Roosevelt bills, which took the power of confirming nominations from the Board of Aldermen.—At that time the politicians raised this same cry that democratic institutions were in danger, &c.;—but to-day not one of them would dare to recommend that we return to that system of "deals" and "bargains."

Unfortunately, as I have mentioned, the Board's power for evil was revived in the same year, by the fatal gift of the power to grant franchises; this too has been practically taken from them, after two years' abuse, during which the City has disposed of its most valuable franchises for very inadequate consideration.

The Board at present has no powers of any importance left to it; it can appoint commissioners of deeds,—but it can do little else.—That the City will continue to pay about $50,000 per year for this—is not very probable; no one will probably dare to recommend that the Board be given any new powers or receive again those of which it has been deprived. The practical question is therefore, is this Board to be abolished, or shall an attempt be made to secure more satisfactory representatives by selecting its members in some other manner?

It is true that the present method has the prestige of antiquity; Governor Dongan, two hundred years ago, introduced the charter, granted by James II., which provided that the City should be divided into wards, and one alderman elected from each ward.—The Montgomery charter, in the early part of the last century, confirmed this, with the limitation, that the Aldermen should be elected only by the freeholders in the Ward.—This system continued down to 1804, when by § 2 of chap. 62 the change was made of extending the franchise to all who had paid taxes during the year and "rented a tenement of the yearly value of twenty-five dollars."

At no time, during these two centuries, can it be said, that the Board of Aldermen has been of great credit to the City.—No sooner had Governor Dongan left, than Leisler,— a man who had obtained his influence as Alderman,— plunged the City into turmoil. Passing over the intermediate period, when the Board was chosen only by the real estate owners of the ward, and seems never to have risen over mediocrity, the change of 1804 did not take long to bring trouble in its train.—Soon the interminable changes began of electing Aldermen and Councilmen in Boards of various sizes, and of depriving them of one power after the other and entrusting these to departments and commissioners.

It is not necessary to detail here this weary story,—we know where it has led to, and we hope, has ended.—After this experience of two centuries, it is senseless to tell New York citizens, that this system of electing aldermen from districts is the best possible and that it must continue unchanged.—Any industrious business man or mechanic, who lives in the City of New York, knows that it is impossible for him to make acquaintances in his Aldermanic district, so as to enable him to exercise any influence in the primaries compared with that of the liquor dealer, who spends his whole days and evenings behind his bar, and by dispensing cheap but highly appreciated favors among his impecunious neighbors, gains a power, which assures him control of the primary.—People living in small towns or in the country, can with difficulty appreciate the entire ignorance of each other of next door neighbors in New York City.—But it is something which cannot be changed ; the large number of calls which every man has on his leisure time from his friends, who reside all over the City, make it impossible for him to cultivate the acquaintance of his neighbors, if that were always desirable.—Men in a large City have their acquaintances,— thanks to the ease of rapid transit, scattered over the whole city ; they meet each other in their exchanges, offices, and workshops during the day, and get to know and value each other, although their homes may be miles apart.—The men living in the same district, have no interests as such, in common ; the geographical division of cities is artificial,—copied from rural institutions.—In the country, the people living in the same neighborhood not only know each other, from the permanency of residence, &c.,—but as they cultivate the same soil under the same conditions, their principal crops are generally the same, and consequently when a geographical division of the country is represented, a group of men is represented united according to their most important interests.—In cities, men do not get their living from the earth, but from manufacturing, transporting, &c., its detached products ;—consequently geographical divisions of a city tear men asunder and prevent the great mass of industrious mechanics and business men who know and esteem each other from uniting in the selection of a representative whom they know and honor.—And so long as this unnatural division continues, the liquor dealers and their gangs will continue to rule the City ; that is inevitable.

But let the Legislature give our City the chance of acting in its natural way, as a political unit, and the inhabitants of New York, who hold the commerce of this continent in their grasp, and who are always the first to be appealed to and the first to respond to any appeal to their generosity, will show that they have the sagacity as well as the civic pride, necessary to redeem the reputation of their city government from being a bye-word, and an example of everything that is to be avoided to the inhabitants of two continents,—and will make it worthy of the Empire State.

Owing to fortunate circumstances, the Legislature has given us this unexpected chance,—let it not be the Executive who dashes this cup, which the whole press and citizens of all classes have hailed with such delight,—from our lips.— — —We need a Board in which the Citizens can have confidence; the Board of Estimate and Apportionment is too small to consider properly all the City's vast interests. Only to such a Board,—three of whose members are elected on a general ticket, and the fourth appointed by the Mayor,—could the City finances be confided.—But it cannot supervise all the City departments and bring economical, harmonious administration into the whole; to do that, requires a more numerous body,—one selected from the very best men of the City.—These questions which concern the whole City should be decided by representatives of the whole City;—under the present system a majority in thirteen districts may govern the City, although the opposing majorities in the other eleven districts together with the minorities in the 13 districts first named greatly exceed the total of the majorities in the 13 districts.—For example, if the twenty-four districts contained each 10,000 voters, 6000 voters in 13 districts, or 78,000 voters could elect a majority of the Board and disregard the wishes of 162,000; thus a minority can under the present system rule a majority of over twice its size. Nothing can be more undemocratic or contrary to common sense.—In questions which concern a number of men, they should all vote for the men who are to decide them.—This is done in all partnerships or private corporations. It is unheard of to divide the stockholders or partners into classes, and let each class vote for a representative ; no majority of men would expose themselves to the risk of being ruled by a minority ;—but all the stockholders insist on voting directly for the board of trustees.

If each district had a Board of Aldermen of its own, and each of these Boards elected a representative to the general board, there would be reason in the plan ; but according to all precedent the members of a body which is a political whole, should vote as a whole for the agents who are to attend to the common interests of these individuals.

It is only by abolishing this district system and by electing the Aldermen from the whole city, that a real rule of the majority can be secured, and all who favor this true, democratic principle should therefore sustain the system of electing aldermen on a general ticket from the city at large.

But while the friends of this bill have striven thus earnestly to carry into effect the democratic doctrine, that the majority must rule, they have not forgotten the other democratic doctrine of equal importance that so far as possible every portion of the people should have a chance to be heard in our legislative assemblies ; that every group of men, with important interests in common, should have a chance to plead its cause ; "*audiatur et altera pars*" is a principle as old as civilization.—While therefore we desire election on a general ticket from the whole City, we have also recognized that it would not be fair or even desirable that the minority, which may consist of tens of thousands of citizens, should be without even a voice in our City legislature.

But even, if we had desired it, I could see no chance of passing this bill in the Assembly until I recommended cumulative voting ; no Republican Assembly will pass the bill without it, and, as, one house is generally in the hands of that party, it is useless to hope for a bill, without some such provision. But although a Democrat, I do not believe that it would be for the welfare of the City or of the Party, that the Board should be composed exclusively of Democrats.—The experience of all political parties is that when either has an overwhelming majority it does not long retain power. We must have election on a general ticket, and this can be fair only if cumulative voting is allowed.

As to the practical working of this bill, I will only cite the Journal of the Constitutional Convention of Illinois, in favor of cumulative voting.—The question was subsequently submitted to the people and adopted, and is now in successful operation in that State.

Journal of the Constitutional Convention, State of Illinois, 1870.—Report of the Committee on Electoral and Representative Reform (p. 414) :

> "If a voter may now cast three votes for three candidates, why should he not be permitted to give his three votes to one candidate? or two votes to one, and one vote for a second candidate? or to divide them equally between two candidates?
>
> What useful purpose is served by this inhibition on the volition of the citizen? By what right or authority does the agent dictate to his principal, how he shall distribute his votes? If the people are sovereign they should be left free to dispose of their votes as seemeth good in their sight. The only possible motive that can be adduced for requiring the elector to cast but one vote for each candidate in a triple district, is to enable the stronger party to elect three members and to prevent the weaker party from electing any. This too closely resembles the gamblers' game, wherein the parties play for the whole stake, the winner gaining all and the loser losing all. And the same temptations to the commission of frauds, and cheating, exist in both games.
>
> The object of the unrestricted ballot is to enlarge the power and privilege of the voter. Instead of obliging him to distribute

his votes, it gives him the option to do so, or to concentrate them and cast a "plumper" for his favorite candidate. ...

The adoption of this great reform would do much towards abating the baseful spirit of partisan animosity, and removing the temptations and opportunities which now exist for the corrupt use of money at elections; much to prevent the deliberate frauds on the purity of the ballot box, becoming so alarming and frequent.

It will also tend powerfully to relieve the voter from the despotism of party caucuses, and at the same time constrain party leaders to exercise more care in selecting candidates for lawmakers. ... It will enable virtuous citizens to elect the ablest and purest men in their midst, and secure to the legislative councils a larger measure of popular confidence and respect.

The increased power of the voter under the liberty conferred by the proposed amendment, may be thus contrasted with the existing restrictions. A citizen may now cast one vote for A, B and C. If he erases A from his ticket, he loses one third of his voting power. If he also erases B, only one third of it remains. But under the free ballot, he may distribute his voting power in any of the following ways: &c. (examples given). ... Thus by this system, the citizen remains in possession of his complete franchise, and at the same time the theory of democratic government is reduced to practice, and the minority through the agents of their personal choice, speaks, argues, protests and votes in the law-making body."

As I understand that the gentlemen from the Reform Club have prepared an argument in favor of the practical merits of cumulative voting, I now pass to the question of constitutionality.

Here we must remember, that we are discussing whether an act of the Legislature is contrary to any provision of the State constitution; it is not necessary to show, as in the case of an act of Congress, that the Constitution has expressly conferred the power to pass the act in question.

People *vs.* Flagg (46 N. Y., 401).

"All legislative power is conferred on the Senate and Assembly, and if an act is within the legitimate exercise of that power it is valid, unless some restriction or limitation can be found in the Constitution itself.

The distinction between the United States Constitution and our State Constitution is that the former confers upon Congress certain specified powers only, while the latter confers upon the Legislature all legislative power. In the one case, the powers, specifically granted, can only be exercised. In the other all powers, not prohibited, may be exercised."

People *ex rel.* Williams *vs.* Dayton (55 N. Y. 380.

"It must be born in mind that all legislative power has been granted by the Constitution to the Senate and Assembly, and their acts are held to be valid unless restrained by some provision of the instrument."

Bank of Chenango *vs.* Brown (26 N. Y., 467).

People *ex rel.* Williams *vs.* Dayton (55 N. Y., 386).

"Again it is insisted that the Legislature have, for a long time, acted upon the construction claimed by the appellants, and that the executive officers of the State, in pursuance of its mandate, have acquiesced in such construction....

This argument in a government like that of Great Britain, where the constitution consists entirely of precedents and usages would be conclusive; but in one where the paramount law consists of a written constitution, solemnly enacted by the people, for the purpose of organizing the department of government, defining and limiting their respective powers, like that of this State. it is entitled to but little weight.

Here whenever the validity of a legislative act is challenged as unauthorized or prohibited by the Constitution, reference must be had to the instrument itself to determine the question......"

Lemon *vs.* People (20 N. Y., 602).

"Every sovereign State has a right to determine by its laws the condition of all persons who may at any time be within its jurisdiction....

What has been said as to the right of a sovereign State to determine the status of persons within its jurisdiction applies to the States of this Union, except as it has been modified or restrained by the Constitution of the United States" (cases cited).

People *vs.* Draper (15 N. Y., 543).

"Plenary power in the Legislature, for all purposes of civil government is the rule, a prohibition to exercise a particular power is an exception. In inquiring therefore, whether a given statute is constitutional, it is for those who question its validity, to show that it is forbidden."

There is nothing in the State Constitution which prohibits the Legislature from authorizing cumulative voting; on the contrary full power over this subject is expressly given to the Legislature.—Section two in Article X provides: "*All city*, town and village *officers*, whose election or appointment is not provided for by this constitution *shall be elected by the electors of such cities*, towns and villages *or of some division thereof*, or appointed by such authorities thereof *as the Legislature shall designate for that purpose.*"

The leading case on this section is that of People *ex rel.* Furman *vs.* Clute (50 N. Y., 459), affirmed in People *ex rel.* Hatfield *vs.* Comstock (78 N. Y., 361), in which the Court of Appeals held, that this section authorized the Legislature to limit the class of persons, from whom a person could be selected to fill a county office. The court says: "And the power is reserved to the Legislature to direct whether by election or appointment shall be made the choice of all county officers, the mode of the choice of whom is not provided for by the Constitution (Const. Art. X, § 2)."

The Legislature is therefore not only not prohibited from providing for city elections in such manner as it may deem best,—but is expressly authorized so to do.

Under the letter of Constitution it may provide for the election of county officers by some division of the electors.— It is not said that this must be a division according to geographical lines ; but any fraction or quota may be directed to elect officers, to the exclusion of others,— if we claim a strict construction of the constitution.

The Legislature has also frequently exercised this power, in providing for minority representation in various ways; see § 1, Chapter 590, laws of 1857 ; § 1, Chapter 321, laws of 1858 ; §§ 6 and 7, Chapter 138, laws of 1870.

Moreover, Article XIII, § 2, providing for the calling of future constitutional conventions, contains a precisely similar direction to the Legislature, as to the election of delegates to such convention. The Constitution provides, that "the Legislature at its next session shall provide by law for the election of delegates to such convention."—In pursuance of this authority the Legislature, by Chapter 194, of laws of 1867, provided :

> "Thirty of said delegates shall be chosen for the state at large, and may be voted for by all the electors therein as such electors are hereinafter designated, except that no elector shall vote for more than sixteen of said delegates at large."

In pursuance of this call, the constitutional Convention was elected, met, proposed various amendments, which were submitted to the people ; among these was Article VI, providing for an elective judiciary, which was adopted and under it our judges now hold office.—The question of the constitutionality of the act last cited, was very fully discussed in Green *vs.* Shumwah (39 N. Y., 418), in regard to the requirement of a test oath from all voters,—but not a word was said against the propriety or constitutionality of minority representation.

The New York charter of 1873 provided also for minority representation, directing among other things, that there should be six aldermen at large, but that no voter should vote for more than four candidates.—This law continued in force until its repeal in 1882. A question was raised as to its constitutionality, which always excited more of ridicule than of anxiety, on the ground that the law violated § 1, of Art. II, of the Constitution, which provides, that "every male citizen.... shall be entitled to vote.... for all officers that now are or hereafter may be elective by the people."

The constitutionality of the act was in effect maintained by the Special and General Term in the First Department, and in the Court of Appeals this case was dismissed on the ground that the complainants had not been prevented from voting for more than four Aldermen, and consequently had no cause of action.

See People *ex rel.* Angerstein *vs.* Kenny (96 N. Y., 294).

No objection of that kind could even be started against cumulative voting, as provided in this bill,—because no citizen is prohibited from voting for all of the Aldermen to be elected, if he wish so to do ;—and consequently this act is within both the language of this article of the Constitution and of the language of the Court of Appeals.

I examined the very point before I drew the amendment to Senator Daly's bill, providing for cumulative voting.

If however it were necessary to argue the question more fully, it could easily be shown that this § 1, of Art. II, referred only to the election of officers by the people of the whole State.—It was the burning question in the Constitutional Convention of 1821, to remove the requirement of the constitution of 1777, that all voters for the Assembly and Senate should be land-owners.

This was accomplished by this section,—but in all the long debates not a word is said about the election of county or city officers.

In the Constitution of 1846 substantially the same section was again adopted,—together with the additional § 2, of Art. X, above cited, expressly authorizing the Legislature to designate the manner of electing the city and county officers.

The chartered privileges of a city were held to be sacred in those days; thus the elder Governor Clinton and the majority of the Council of Revision had disapproved of a bill altering the franchise in New York City, on the ground that "charters of incorporation containing grants and privileges were not to be essentially affected without the consent of the parties or without due process of law."

The Constitution of 1821 moreover particularly povides, in § 14 of Art. VII., that "*nothing contained in this Constitution* . . . . shall annul any charters to bodies politic and corporate by him or them (the King of Great Britain or persons acting under his authority) made . . . . *or shall affect any such grants or charters made by this State, etc.*" The Constitution of 1846 contains a similar provision.

At the time when the Constitution of 1821 was adopted, the election in New York City of charter officers was regulated by Chapter 62 of the Laws of 1804; this law prescribed requirements for voters, differing from those of the Constitution; for example, a residence of six months in the State was sufficient to entitle a person to vote for charter officers, while the Constitution required a residence of one year.

If this § 1 of Art. II. of the Constitution applied to charter officers, the law concerning election of charter officers, so far as it varied from the Constitution, must have been void. But immediately after the adoption of the Constitution the following act was passed:

Chapter 223 of the Laws of 1822. "*Whereas*, The Mayor, Aldermen and Commonalty of the City of New York, by their petition, under their corporate seal, have prayed the Legislature to pass the hereinafter contained provisions, Therefore, be it enacted by the people, etc. . . . .

§ 6. That *every person qualified by the charter of the said city, to vote for charter officers, and* every person qualified to vote in any of the wards of the said city, for members of the Assembly of this State, by the Constitution of the State of New

York, as amended, *shall be authorized to vote for such charter officers* in the ward where he actually resides and not elsewhere."

Two years later a similar act was passed: Chapter 155, of 1824.

"An act to alter the organisation of the Common Council of the the City of New York.

§ 9. *Every person qualified by the charter of the said city to vote for charter officers*, and every person qualified to vote in any of the wards of the said city, for members of the assembly of this state by the constitution, shall be authorized to vote for such charter officers in the ward where he actually resides and not elsewhere; and that no other person shall be authorized to vote at any such election.

§ 11. That all the provisions of this act shall be null ... unless the same shall be approved by a majority of the votes of the electors of the City of New York."

It is therefore plain that these Legislatures did not consider the broader franchise allowed by the act of 1804 to be affected by the Constitution. Frequent subsequent references to the qualification of voters under the city charter occur. Thus Amendment Number Six to the Constitution of 1821, adopted a few years subsequently, provides that in the City of New York "the electors thereof qualified *to vote for the other charter officers* of the said city" shall annually choose the Mayor. Similar references are found in Chapter 155 of laws of 1824 and Chapter 23 of laws of 1834. The courts have unanimously held that the acts passed to carry into effect this § 1, of Article II., of the Constitution, do not apply to charter elections.

Thus Chapter 130 of laws of 1842, providing for general elections, re-enacts § 1, of Art. II., of the Constitution, and declares that no court shall be open on the day when such election shall be held. In the following case it was decided that this act did not apply to charter elections.

Matter of the Election Law (7 Hill, 194).

"A doubt was suggested whether under the election law of 1842 the court could properly be held open. In consequence of this suggestion he (the Chief Justice) had looked into the statute and was of the opinion that it did not apply to town and charter elections.... The elections particularly provided for, and which are held in pursuance of the chapter, are general and special elections for the choice of State, district or county officers, and no others. It is true that the act provides for the choice of Inspectors of Elections at town meetings and charter elections. Those meetings and elections, however, are not held in pursuance of the law in question; *but under other laws specially providing when and how they shall be held and conducted.*"

See also: People *vs.* Tripp (4 N. Y. Legal Observer, 344); Wheeler *vs.* Bartlett (1 Edw. Eh. p. 323); Redfield *vs.* Florence (2 E. D. Smith, 342); Pitkin *vs.* McNair (56 Barb., 75.) The qualifications for voters for township officers appear also not to have been affected by the Constitution; —see Rev. Stat., p. 339, § 1; § 5 of laws of 1823, p. 207.

Having thus attempted to meet the arguments which may be advanced against the constitutionality of the bill, I will close with a few remarks in answer to the suggestion which may perhaps be made that while this bill may not be against the letter of our Constitution, it is nevertheless an innovation and against the spirit of our institutions, especially that of universal suffrage, which all democrats must value so highly.

I believe that cumulative voting is an essential part of true universal suffrage.

Whence did we get universal suffrage? Not from England.—The writs for election of members to parliament left it entirely undecided how each borough would select its two representatives. To quote an authority from the last century: Heywood on Borough Elections (1797), Chapter VI; On the Electors for cities and boroughs in general (p. 171).

"The right of voting for representatives of cities and boroughs is not (as of counties) regulated by any one fixed rule, which uniformly pervades the whole kingdom, but inquiry must be made after the acts of parliament, charters, or last determinations affecting each particular place, and the local usage prevailing there. After having shown that the tenants in ancient demesne and in burgage, were probably the most ancient classes of voters, it is not unreasonable to conclude, that many, if not all of the present rights of voting, however remote their connexion or analogy may at first appear, were derived originally *from tenure*, as the parent stock."

In none of the United Sates did universal suffrage prevail at the time of the Revolution, and the United States Constitution said not a word about extending that right. It was practically unknown for nearly a generation afterwards. Universal suffrage is therefore originally neither an English nor an American doctrine; it was introduced by the Democratic party, in State after State, under the influence of the example of France and the suggestions of Thomas Jefferson— in this State thanks chiefly to Martin Van Buren.—What was the universal suffrage which Thos. Jefferson saw during his long residence in France?—The Assemblée Nationale of 1789 provided, that each department should elect as many representatives as it has thousands of inhabitants.—The Republic of 1848 introduced a similar system; the present Republic in 1875 instituted it afresh, and although this was repealed, it has been again established and is now in force in France, with cumulative voting—thanks to the last gigantic effort of Gambetta.—It is for this principle of the *scrutin du liste*, as opposed to that of the *scrutin d'arrondissement*, that we are contending; we ask for a similar election for a number of representatives from a large district, on a general ticket, with cumulative voting.

The opponents of this measure have expressed the fear that the people could not be trusted to exercise the franchise under this system; but this argument should have little weight with a Democrat.

It was this system of election of a number of representatives on a general ticket from a large district which Jefferson saw in operation when he wrote to David Hartley: "I have no fear, but that the result of our experiment will be, that men may be trusted to govern themselves without a master. Could the contrary of this be proved, I should conclude either that there was no God or that he was a malevolent being." This plan has always been bitterly opposed by all the enemies of Republican France: anarchists, imperialists, royalists and small politicians.

We hold with Gambetta's declaration on November 24, 1875:

> "The laws which regulate are as essential, are as fundamental for the future of society as those which established it."

All that we are asking for is that the one essential element, which is lacking to make universal suffrage what it was expected to be, be added, and that this principle be practically applied, in its full strength, on the plan of those who designed and originated it. For a fuller statement on this subject I beg leave to refer to my pamphlet on "Universal Suffrage in Cities," which I submit herewith, in which I also attempt to show the necessity of electing representatives to the Legislature from cities, on the plan now advocated for Aldermen.

What greater glory can a democratic Governor have than of initiating the final stage in the completion of this grand democratic doctrine?—Unless some wise change is made, it is greatly to be feared that in our city it cannot maintain its hold on the affections of our people.—We must abolish this division into districts—this remnant of British feudal and of federalist institutions, but this can not and ought not to be done without a provision for minority representation.

All that this bill asks for is the true rule of the majority, the representation of the whole people, the perfection and preservation of universal suffrage;—the completion of the work begun in this State by Martin Van Buren.

Progress and Robbery.

THREE AMERICAN ANSWERS TO HENRY GEORGE.

A PROPERTY-OWNER'S ANSWER.

The candidacy of Mr. Henry George for the mayoralty is in one way peculiar and appears to me to demand a different treatment in this Club, from the usual mere indorsement or refusal to indorse.

Mr. George is known personally to but few of our citizens; it is only through his books that we can obtain information as to his character, sympathies and intellectual ability. As most of the members of this Club are busy men, and yet must desire to be informed on this subject, I thought it might be acceptable, if I submitted to you the result of my examination of his works, especially as it will consist largely in quotations, showing his opinions on the salient points of his theory.

Mr. George, moreover, represents an idea;—for no one can deny that but for his book on "Progress and Poverty" he would not have been nominated for this office. He is not nominated merely because it is believed that he will make a good administrative officer, but because it is hoped that his election will in some way conduce to the realization of a whole theory of political economy, applicable not only to our City, but to the State and Nation. That this theory is of sufficient importance to deserve the careful consideration of this Club, is evidenced, I consider, by the general interest which this nomination of its representative has excited among all citizens.

Among the masses of the people every one knows that a large number of persons who have heretofore voted the Democratic ticket are considering whether they will not vote for Mr. George, or have already made up their minds so to do; it is the same with the Republicans.

The manner in which he has been nominated is another matter which should attract the attention of this Club. He has not been nominated by politicians, but by a great class of our population; he represents in many ways a revolt against present political methods; he is brought forward by a combination of organizations whose entrance in the field of politics has long been looked forward to by our citizens with mingled feelings of desire and dread; he has been placed at the head of a force whose movements statesmen and politicians have long been studying and prognosticating, and which, whatever may be the result of this election, will remain a power for good or evil in the political horizon for a long time to come, which both political parties will have to consider in their calculations, and which may be so strong as to retain permanently the elements that may be attracted to it from either party in this campaign. What theories then does the standard-bearer of this new movement represent?

It seems to me that this Club should look this matter in the face at once, and consider whether the principles, which Henry George represents, vary from the teachings of Democracy, and whether there is anything that prevents a Democrat from supporting him as a candidate.

Even if these questions were not forced upon us at this time, the examination of the doctrines taught in "Progress and Poverty" appear to me to be a fitting subject for our careful consideration, whether we are inclined to approve or disapprove of them, in view of the great spread which this book has attained both in this country and in England In this country over a hundred editions are said to have been printed, and it has been translated, I believe, into all the languages of Europe. Learned societies have debated its theories and clubs have been formed to put them into practice. Very few books can boast of the reception of this work,—or of having immediately influenced so many minds in its favor. Another reason for considering this work is that it is necessary in order to understand the full and correct meaning of the platform adopted by the Trade and Labor Organizations of New York, and on which Mr. George stands.

The first section condemns "the system which compels men to pay their fellow-creatures for the use of God's gifts to all," although it does not define what that "system" is; and the second section states that "we aim at the abolition of all laws which give to any class of citizens advantages either judicial, financial, industrial or political, that are not equally shared by all others,"—but the statutes referred to are not cited. This platform was adopted after the receipt of a letter from Mr. George in which he promised conditionally to accept the nomination, and as it is understood that he has virtually accepted it, we can go safely to his works to ascertain the meaning which he, at all events, puts upon this language, and which he will consider himself justified to follow in his official acts, if elected. And no one can deny that a vote for Henry George will be construed as an indorsement to some extent of his theories. What is this system and what are these laws which are to be abolished?

Mr. George has certainly been straight-forward and consistent; in his four books: "Progress and Poverty," "Social Problems," "The Irish Land Question" and "Protection and Free Trade," he emits no uncertain sound.

As the Roman Senator, when suddenly awakened, exclaimed: "*Carthago delenda est*," so Mr. George would, I believe, in similar circumstances exclaim in the final words of his closing chapter in "Protection and Free Trade:" "Private property in land is doomed."

It is this cry with which he first startled the world in "Progress and Poverty": "We must therefore substitute for the individual ownership of land a common ownership. We must make land common property," p. 295.

In his "Social Problems" he says, on page 276: "There is no escape from it. We must make land common property."

In the "Land Question" he states: "In the very nature of things, land cannot rightfully be made individual property. This principle is absolute," p. 38.

It is therefore this system of private ownership of land, and the laws which sustain this system, which the delegates of the Trade and Labor Organizations of New York, in conference assembled, declare it to be their aim to abolish, and as the first step in that direction, they have nominated Mr. George for Mayor of New York City. And no one can deny that if this was their object, they have made a wise choice in their standard-bearer. He gives not merely an intellectual assent to the proposition, but no one can doubt his thorough sincerity and fiery zeal.

His work entitled "Protection and Free Trade," published in 1885 is as outspoken in its denunciations as his "Progress and Poverty," written in 1877.

In the former he says: "Property in land is as indefensible as property in man," (p. 349) and "the robber that takes all that is left is private property in land," (p. 285); in the later he says: "If chattel slavery be unjust then is private property in land unjust," (p. 312). In his "Land Question" he says, on page 36: "Here is a system which robs the producers of wealth as remorselessly and far more regularly and systematically than the pirate robs the merchantman."

In his "Social Problems" he says: "Did you ever see a pail of swill given to a pen of hungry hogs? That is human society as it is," (p. 102).

And, indeed, extravagant as this language may sound, when one reads the sombre pages on which he paints the horrors and misery of poverty and contrasts it with the extravagance of wealth, in language and with pathos, which has been rarely surpassed, one feels more than half inclined to adopt Mr. George's plan or any measure, no matter how radical, if there was only some prospect of improvement.

But Mr. George does not confine himself to an appeal to our sentiments; he recognizes, of course, that no matter how readily we agree as to the misery and unjustifiable inequality now existing, he must still show that his proposed remedy will lead to an improvement, and also that it can be adopted without acting contrary to the precepts of justice.—Thus, he says in his "Progress and Poverty": "If private property in land be just, then is the remedy I propose a false one; if on the contrary, private property in land be unjust, then is this remedy the true one," (p. 299.)

As to the justice of ownership of things other than land Mr. George is pronounced; in his "Social Problems," he says, on pays 278: "What more preposterous than the treatment of land as individual property? In every essential land differs from those things which being the product of human labor are rightfully property. It is the creation of God ; they are produced by man."

It is on this distinction that he bases his whole system. In his chapter entitled "Injustice of private property in land," he says (p. 307): "The right to exclusive ownership of anything of human production is clear. No matter how many the hands through which it has passed, there was at the beginning of the line human labor—some one who, having procured or produced it by his exertions, had to it a clear title as against all the rest of mankind, and which could justly pass from one to another by sale or gift. But at the end of what string of conveyances or grants can be shown or supposed a like title to any part of the material universe ?"

I think that such a title can be shown to every piece of land in the State of New York fit for human use.

There is no reason for the division between personal and real property, on the ground that the former is the product of man and the latter created by God. God created personal property as certainly as he did real. As Mr. George says in his "Social Problems" (p. 182): "Man has no power to bring something out of nothing. He cannot create an atom of matter."

Man can fashion things after they are detached from the soil, and combine them, so that they will affect every one of our senses in a new manner; but is any such change greater than that from a piece of the forest primeval to a Fifth Avenue lot?

Did it require no labor to drain the swamps, cut the trees and blast the rocks on this Island of Manhattan, before it assumed its present form, which Mr. George and his friends are now content to assume as their place of residence? Was not similar work required on every field in the State? Ask a farmer, who has reduced a ten-acre lot to an arable condition, or the builder, who has blasted the rock from a city lot, whether Mr. George is correct when he says, in his "Social Problems," on page 85: "When land increases in value it does not mean that its owner has added to the general wealth."

According to Mr. George's own definitions, land can be held as property, because it is no more fit for human use without human labor, than any piece of personal property, and it is as senseless to say of one part of the material universe it can be produced by man without God, as it is of any other.

It is true that Mr. George does not overlook this point of human labor connected with land, but he says on the page last cited: "It is a title only to the improvements and not to the land itself." Should he not then also say the same thing concerning a diamond, for instance, which a lapidary has cut and polished: "All I can justly claim is the value given by these exertions. They give me no right to the diamond itself." And yet Mr. George claims that as to personal property one can have ownership.

Quote to the same farmer or builder the definition of property, as given in this chapter under consideration, "As a man belongs to himself, so his labor when put in concrete form belongs to him," and ask him whether he does not think that the definition would entitle him to claim property in the lot as much as in the wood or the stone which he removes from it, and it would take even more than Mr. George's ingenuity to get a negative answer from him.

We are not now arguing the question of compensation for improvements, which we will consider later, but examining the correctness of the distinction which Mr. George makes between property in land and property in other things. If there be no such broad distinction, as to require that the former should be taken and the latter left, as Mr. George so earnestly demands, the question of compensation, in case we should take the land, need not be considered. Unless this radical difference be proven, he might with equal propriety discuss in his book the compensation to be given for improvements to personal property. Having thus, in my opinion, shown that Mr. George's distinction between personal property, as the product of man, and real property, as the creation of God, is untenable, and that consequently his whole theory is indefensible, as he has expressly based it on this claim to justice, let us briefly consider the question of justice, without reference to Mr. George's book.

How long has this work been going on in this State and City before they acquired a form, which induces Mr. George and his friends to take up their abode therein and even to desire to have an interest in it? Where were these gentlemen or their ancestors during the two centuries during which this struggle with animate and inanimate foes was going on? Did they take part in the Indian wars? Did they fight at Saratoga, or endure the horrors of the seven years' war? Did they struggle for municipal rights against the New Netherlands Company, or assist in planning the Constitution of 1777? Were not their ancestors the men who staid comfortably in Europe until America was prepared and put in order—until the human, animal and material foes were overcome, and now that a passage can be made in a week, and steerage fares cost perhaps twenty dollars—which is often advanced to them by Americans—they sail over here and, not satisfied with our broad naturalization laws, then complain: "American citizenship confers no right to American soil," (Social Problems, p. 146). The Report of the Charity Organization Society (which Mr. George cites to prove the existing misery) shows that over 80 per cent. of beggars, whose cases were investigated, were not born in America.

No matter how absurd this claim may now seem to us, it is one deserving of careful attention—in fact, is not to be wondered at: our Saxon ancestors once did the same thing and thus gained their English homes. It was the Britons who invited the Saxons over from the Continent to fight the Picts, and supported them and took them into their pay, until they finally so increased in number that they took possession of the land of their former employers. Human nature has not changed very much, and that they come over in Cunarders, instead of in dragon ships or coracles, does not make their demand for the land of the former inhabitants essentially different. I believe that the true character of this movement, which is just beginning, should be understood by our real estate owners and their friends, so that the contest shall be a fair and open one, and that the leaders of neither side shall increase their forces or diminish hat of their adversary by false pretenses of justice, disinterestedness, etc.

If one wished to descend to his style of language could not the terms "robber" and "pirate" be flung back with perfect propriety?

I happen to have the correspondence of James Duane (an ancestor of mine), who settled the township of Duanesburgh, in Schenectady County, with his agents, extending from about 1770 to 1790. I would like to show that correspondence to anyone who claims that land is the free gift of God to man and can be used like air and water, without the expenditure of labor. Mr. Duane spent the proceeds of a large professional income, together with what was, in those days, considerable inherited property, upon building roads, dams, mills, etc., through that region, so as to make it accessible to his tenants; he advanced them money, as is shown by the continual begging letters, all of them implying confidence in his generosity or gratitude for his assistance; there is not one implying any dislike or harsh feeling; a great part of the letters consist in explanations by the agent why the various tenants did not meet their obligations, or requests for money to carry out improvements or maintain those already begun, which seemed very liable to dilapidation. After representing the State of New York in every Congress during the Revolutionary War, and serving as first Mayor of this City after the war, until the Union was formed, and then as first Judge of the United States District Court of New York, he gave up the latter position, and moved up there and devoted himself entirely to care of this land until his death. Would he have done this, if his descendants were to have had no interest in what was then a wilderness? And if he had not done it, how long would that land have remained uncultivated?

I believe that the history of any portion of this State, if known, would be very much the same; and if any one will consult one of the latest books on the history of land, "The English Village Community," by Frederic Seebohm

(London, 1883), he will see that in England the theory of an original cultivation of the land by a community of independent farmers (on which, on page 331 of "Progress and Poverty," Mr. George bases his historical argument) is a myth, and that the new land was then also settled by some man of means advancing to dependents the subsistence and implements required during the hard struggle of rendering land arable. Mr. Seebohm says in his conclusion (p. 438) on the village land system: "The equality in its yardlands, and the single succession which preserved this equality, we have found to be apparently not marks of an original freedom, not of an original allodial allotment on the German mark system, but of a settled serfdom under a lordship—a semi-servile tenancy implying a mere usufruct, theoretically only for life or at will, and carrying with it no inherent rights of inheritance. But this serfdom, as we have seen reason to believe, was, to the masses of the people, not a degradation, but a step upward out of a once more general slavery. Certainly during the 1200 years over which the direct English evidence extends, the tendency has been towards more and more freedom." And Mr. Seebohm implies that the same facts probably existed in other early agricultural communities. Mr. George based his views solely on what he saw in the Great West, where prairies are said to be almost ready for the plow with but little preliminary labor; and upon the rapid increase of real estate values in California, consequent upon the discovery of gold. From these extraordinary circumstances he has evolved a theory which he believes to be of general application and to which he still adheres, although his subsequent travels and education might have been expected to have widened and corrected his views on this plain matter of history.

He says, in page 83 of his "Social Studies: "When land increases in value it does not mean that its owner has added to the general wealth. . . . Increase of land values simply means that the owners, by virtue of appropriation of something that existed before man was, have the power of taking a larger share of the wealth produced by other people's labor." However applicable these remarks may be to other parts of the country, and though they may show that the laws concerning the pre-emption of different kinds of public lands should have varied, they do not apply to this State, with its comparatively rugged soil and thick woods.

What have real estate owners done for the State of New York? Under the Constitution of 1777, only those in the possession of land could vote, and to the Senate only landowners were admitted. It was the landowners of New York who enabled that State to meet every requisition made upon it by the Continental Congress for supplies, men and money —the only one of the thirteen States of which that can be said.

After forty years, the landowners peaceably of their own accord gave up this privilege, and established practically universal suffrage, through the Constitutional Convention of 1826, although there were even then men who foresaw the future. Thus Chancellor Kent said, on page 115 of "Proceedings:"

"It is to protect this important class of the community that the Senate should be preserved. It should be the representative of the landed interest, and its security against the caprice of the motley assemblage of paupers, emigrants, journeymen manufacturers, and those undefinable classes of inhabitants which a State and city like ours is calculated to invite. This is not a fancied alarm.

Universal suffrage jeopardizes property, and puts it into the power of the poor and profligate to control the affluent."

He was answered by Mr. Root: "We have no different estates having different interests, necessary to be guarded from encroachment by the watchful eye of jealousy . . . We are all the same estate, all commoners . . . These powerful checks may be necessary between different families possessing adverse interests, but can never be salutary among brothers of the same family, whose interests are similar," (p. 116.)

What would have been the action of that Convention, if Mr. George's language had been heard in it? Would he and his friends now be voters? Does he subscribe to the honeyed phrases of that advocate of universal suffrage, or are those former "brothers" now called robbers and pirates, among whom must be included of course Washington, Franklin, Madison, Jackson and probably every name which Americans have been taught to revere.

I would pass now from the main point of Mr. George's theory, assuming that it has appeared that Mr. George's distinction between real and personal property is baseless, and that property in the one is as sacred as in the other, and that consequently the question of compensation for improvements on land, taken by the public, will not arise, because the land may not be taken. But in order to give a more complete view of Mr. George's theory, let us consider for a moment his plan for compensation.

He assumes that there are two kinds of improvements to land, for one of which only compensation is to be made.

He says on page 308 of "Progress and Poverty:" "There are improvements which in time become indistinguishable from the land itself. Very well; then the title to the improvements becomes blended with the title to the land; the individual right is lost in the common right."

But he says this in the chapter on "injustice of private property in land," in which he has undertaken to show that this common right exists according to the principles of justice; and yet here he assumes that it is already proven and justified, to the negation of the right even of compensation for improvements.—This is a fair specimen of the logical mind of our would-be future Mayor.

But what are these "indistinguishable" improvements; the term is rather vague. Naturally one would suppose that it would include the results of the first attempts to render wild land fit for cultivation or habitation; such as the building of roads, bridges and dams in agricultural lands, and clearing away the stones and other objects, which impede cultivation; and in the city, levelling the ground, making the necessary excavations, etc.—I do not know what else can be intended by these "indistinguishable" improvements.

I would not ask Mr. George whether this is fair or honest, but I would ask him whether it is consistent with giving compensation for any improvements?

Houses and barns, I suppose, would be improvements, if any thing would, whose value is distinguishable from that of the land; but why should the labor spent on the erection of the building be compensated, and not that spent on the preparation of the site or digging the foundation?

The real object of this distinction between these two classes of improvements appears to be to form a loop-hole through which Mr. George can creep, whenever he is pressed on this point, so as to suit the wishes of his interlocutor. But his real spirit with which he would select the "indistinguishable" improvements is shown plainly enough throughout his works. He says in his "Land Question," on page 38: "I have dwelt so long upon this question of compensating landowners, not merely because it is of great practical importance, but because its discussion brings clearly into view the principles upon which the land question in Ireland, or in any other country, can alone be justly and finally settled. In the light of these principles we see that the landowners have no rightful claim either to the tand or to compensation for its resumption by the people, and, further than that, we see that no such rightful claim can ever be created. It would be wrong to pay the present landowners for "their" land at the expense of the people."

On page 36 he says: "Yet we are told. . . . .that this system cannot be abolished without buying off those who profit by it. Was there ever more degrading debasement before a fetish?"

Moreover, who would pay for these improvements, if any were paid for? It would be one landowner who would pay the other, for he contemplates the abolition of all other taxes. He says, on page 281 of "Social Problems:" "Were land treated as the property of the whole people, the ground rent accruing to the community would suffice for public purposes and all other taxation might be dispensed with." Literally his greatest advance towards compensating the landowners consists in robbing Peter to pay Paul.

The last point in Mr. George's theories to which I think it necessary to refer, is his proposed method of accomplishing his great reforms. He says, on page 364 of "Progress and Poverty:" "I do not propose either to purchase or to confiscate private property in land. The first would be unjust; the second, needless. . . . . . .We may safely leave them the shell if we take the kernel. *It is not necessary to confiscate land; it is only necessary to confiscate rent.* . . . . .We already take some rent in taxation. We have only to make some changes in our modes of taxation to take it all." The naiveté of these remarks is refreshing. "Taking property" has a bad name in civilized countries; even professed criminals prefer to avoid it, and to speak of divided the stuff, the boodle or the swag. But if Mr. George thinks that anyone is deceived by this use of terms, it shows that he has great simplicity of mind. Of course this would make the city or the State the landlord, with the accompanying duties and responsibilities; how they would be fulfilled it is needless to explain to gentlemen so well acquainted with the present workings of our government, as the members of this Club. Mr. George says, on page 410: "Government would change its character and would become the administration of a great co-operative society. It would become merely the agency by which the common property was administered for the common benefit."

As to the manner in which the money is to be spent and the benefits to be derived therefrom, Mr. George gives glowing pictures. The Reverend Heber Newton summed the matter up in his speech at the so-called Business Men's Meeting of last week, when he said: "We are going to clear the way for the millenium." Mr. George describes, in his "Social Problems," on page 323, the ordinary farmer, living "with a daily average of two or three hours' work, which more resembled healthy recreation than toil;" that his family "should be able to visit the theatre, or concert or opera as often as they cared to, and occasionally to make trips to other parts of the country or to Europe."

In his argument in favor of free trade, which he also claims can be brought about only through the appropriation of all land, he says, on page 334 of "Protection and Free Trade:" "An English Democrat puts in this phrase the aim of true Free Trade : 'No taxes at all, and a pension to everybody.' . . . . .If this is Socialism, then it is time that Free Trade leads to Socialism."

Is this the language of a practical man ?

We have not time here for me to undertake to show the hopelessness of any real improvement of the condition of the workingmen through these theories ; I would refer you to the criticisms by Mr. John Rae in "Contemporary Socialism" and to Mr. Mallock's book on this subject ; but I would call your attention to this fact, that in his earlier work he promised the Millenium, if his plan were adopted. Thus he says in "Progress and Poverty," on page 295: "To extirpate poverty....we must therefore substitute for the individual ownership of land a common ownership." But in his later book, "Social Problems," he says on page 273: "Yet we might recognize the equal right to the land and tyranny and spoliation be continued, . . . I fully recognize the fact that even after we do this, much will remain to do."

Would it not be well to wait until his plan is complete, before pulling down our present dwelling? How much more "will remain to do," before his glowing phantasies are to become realities? Does this uncertain prophet deserve to be followed by the workingmen into a conflict with the great class of real estate owners and their friends?

I would further call attention to this fact that Mr. George's arguments are nothing new. They bear a strong resemblance to those of Proudhon in his book entitled: "*Qu'est ce que la Propriété?*" to which he answers: "Property is theft." Proudhon claimed that property in movables was as wrong as property in land,—but another Frenchman, Considerant, attempted to draw the same distinctions which Mr. George has drawn between real and personal property, and prove the lawfulness of the latter. Mr. George and Considerant also use very much the same arguments.

Nowhere, however, that I can find, does Mr. George cite Considerant; although he is evidently familiar with French writers, as he has dedicated his "Protection and Free Trade" "to the memory of those illustrious Frenchmen of a century ago, Quesnay, Turgot, Mirabeau, Condorcet, Dupont and their fellows, who in night of despotism foresaw the glories of the coming day." Mr. George then proceeds to argue in favor of abolition of property in land,—without mentioning Considerant. It is, of course, possible that Mr. George has so superficially studied this subject that he did not hear of the writings of that author, and that the resemblance in the arguments is purely accidental. It is as probable that a man writing on electricity should not have heard the name of Benjamin Franklin, or on abolition of slavery and should not have heard the name of Abraham Lincoln. But be this as it may, there is nothing new in Mr. George's arguments; they have been promulgated half a century ago by unprincipled Frenchmen in a dozen ways, and the Paris Commune was an attempt to realize them.

If we draw a conclusion as to Mr. George's character from these works, can we conclude anything except that his mind is that of an illogical, unpractical and dangerous fanatic?

At all times progress has had to be on its guard against robbery. We have seen what the system and the laws are which this platform demands shall be abolished. It is true that the Mayor is supposed to be an administrative officer; but cannot the Mayor of New York do something to carry out these principles? In the first place he is a member of the Board of Estimate and Apportionment, which has the power, practically without limitation, of determining the amount of money to be raised each year by taxation. This Board consists of four members; one of them, the President of the Department of Taxes and Assessments, is appointed by the Mayor. Should a vacancy occur in that office, the Mayor might appoint a friend entertaining his views, and they would have one-half the Board. But without that, the tax levy can only be fixed by the unanimous vote of all the four members on each item; every member can veto any item, unless he is satisfied with the appropriation as a whole. Mr. George can, therefore, demand that an immense sum should be raised next year by taxation, or he might by refusing to agree with any items cripple the entire city government. That his power would be immense, of that there can be no doubt.

The Mayor also appoints the Board of Taxes and Assessments, which in turn appoints Deputy Tax Commissioners, who fix the valuation of real estate in their several districts for purposes of taxation.—(Sec. 14 of the Consolidation Act of 1882.)

Even if Mr. George should not appoint directly to these offices, it is well known that with his patronage he could probably influence their appointment, so as to obtain the positions for persons in sympathy with him, and every one knows how easily these officials could change the present valuation of real estate.

Then the chief practical defense of house-owners in this city comes through the summary proceedings, which are executed by the Marshals of the District Courts. These officers are appointed by the Mayor, and, like other city officials, removed only by him. If he should nominate some of his present supporters, fresh from reading his "Social Problems," where, on page 155, he states that certain landlords "are of no more use than so many great ravenous, destructive beasts, packs of wolves, herds of wild elephants, or such dragons as St. George is reported to have killed," and a complaint should be brought before him against a marshal for neglect of duty in a dispossess proceeding,—what attention would it be likely to receive? Behind the marshall, for protection of all property stand the police; what sort of men will Mr. George's Police Commissioners be apt to appoint?

We see, therefore, that a Mayor of New York, with Mr. George's views, might do much to carry them into effect. Probably in no position in the world, under our present laws, could more be done in this direction. It is indeed rare that an enthusiast of that type has a chance to attempt to realize such dreams, and Mr. George will be a good deal less sincere than his book shows him to be, if he does not use this wonderful opportunity to the utmost.

I submit, therefore, that all good citizens should oppose his candidacy.

But particularly, as Democrats, what ought we to do?

The fundamental principle of the Democracy has always been that of admiration and steadfast adherence to the Constitution and laws authorized by that Constitution. What have they to say on this subject?

The United States Constitution declares in the Fifth Amendment: "Nor shall private property be taken for public use without just compensation."

We have seen the important part which landowners played in the formation of the Constitution of this State.

Section 6 of the New York State Constitution is to the same effect, and Sec. 13 of this Constitution says: "All lands within this State are declared to be allodial, so that, subject only to the liability to escheat, the entire and absolute property is vested in the owners, according to the nature of their respective estates."

Section 8, of II. Revised Statutes, p. 719, declares: "Every citizen of the United States is capable of holding lands within this State, and of taking the same by descent, devise or purchase."

This indeed is no new doctrine; it was imbedded in Magna Charta, which declared that no freeman shall be disseised or divested of his freehold, or of his liberties or free customs, but by the judgment of his peers, or by the law of the land. Blackstone, in his "Commentaries," Vol. I., p. 129, declares that the three absolute rights of individuals are: "The right of personal security, the right of personal liberty, and the right of prrivate property;" and Chancellor Kent, in Vol. II., p. 1. of his "Commentaries," uses the same language. Elliott's "Constitutional Debates," on the adoption of the United States Constitution in the different States are full of allusions to the protection of property in land, which this Constitution would afford.

That our Constitution and laws recognize no principle as more fundamental and sacred than that of private property in land is therefore undeniable.

But Mr. George would perhaps say that he does not demand that the title to land should be taken, but only the rent, and therefore that he does not take property.

He might claim that property meant the thing which is the object of ownership and not the aggregate of rights which an owner has over the thing, so that property was not taken when an owner was deprived of one of these essential rights, such as that of rent, but only when the thing itself was removed or interfered with. But the recent long line of cases in the suits against the Elevated Railroads have settled in this State that property means the aggregate of rights and not the thing owned. Probably the most recent decision is that of the Court of Appeals in the matter of Jacobs (98 N. Y., 105).

"The constitutional guaranty that no person shall be deprived of his property without due process of law may be violated without the physical taking of property for public or private use. Property may be destroyed, or its value may be annihilated . . . any law which destroys it or its value, or takes away any of its essential attributes, deprives the owner of his property."

However, Mr. George would hardly dare to make this contention, in view of his oft repeated use of the term property, in its correct sense, as defined by the courts; thus, on page 343, of " Protection and Free Trade," he says: "The only way to abolish private property is by the way of taxation. That way is clear and straightforward."

Since then this direct conflict exists between Mr. George's opinions and the "aims" of his platform on the one hand, and the Constitution and the laws on the other, and since it is also by no means clear which of these "aims" are at once to be put into practice, and since the peculiar boast of the Democracy has always been its conservative strict adherence to the Constitution, I do not see how any Democrat can support Mr. George.

However, I do not see how Mr. George can accept this office, if elected. How can he swear to support the Constitution and laws of this State as they now exist, while he maintains the views expressed in his works?—No matter how he may hedge in his letter of acceptance, I do not believe that he can, if he would, free his mind from the passions which these years of controversy have engendered, and see to the administration of these laws, so abhorrent to him, according to their letter and their spirit. If he were running for the Constitutional Convention, this objection would not exist; but to attempt to fill the position of Mayor, without abolishing our present system, but according to the true meaning of the laws now in force, ought to be thoroughly abhorrent to him, if he means half of what he has said. — I can not imagine his taking that oath, without mental reservations, which would make it practically perjury;—and I believe that those who approve of his making such an attempt and aid him in it, by their votes, are not much better than accomplices before the act.

Finally, I wish to state that these remarks have been made with no feeling of hostility to the workingmen. In my humble way I have for years, by various publications, done what I could to induce them to go into politics; I believe it is a necessary movement, and in time will be a salutary one. But I object to this great movement, the most important one which will probably occur in our generation, instead of being utilized in a practical manner for the benefit of all, being turned aside to attack one class of our fellow-citizens. Henry George says, in his "Progress and Poverty," (p. 282): "Nor in the struggle of endurance must it be forgotten who are the real parties pitted against each other. . . . . .It is laborers on the one side and the owners of land on the other." This will not be the first of these conflicts. The history of the Dark Ages—of the 13th, 14th and 15th centuries—is red with the blood spilt in the cities of Europe in the fights between the trade unions and the real estate owners; every man who reads that history must feel it his duty to do all in his power to prevent the kindling of such a conflict here.

While we can all hope that the contingency of such fearful contests is still remote, we must recognize that even this peaceful strife at the polls of these two great classes prevents their uniting their forces and righting the many wrongs which they jointly suffer. I do not say that this contest has been engineered by the railroad kings, politicians and monopolists, who thrive in the present disorganized state of society, but I do say that nothing could have happened more opportunely for them, and that if they can only fan the flame, they have gained a new lease of life. Moreover, with our system of government the danger of diffusion of these ideas among persons who have not opportunity or ability to thoroughly examine them and see their fallacy, presents a great danger, which all good citizens should oppose. Mr. George's arguments apply to personal property as well as to real; a movement started against the latter cannot be stopped there; in all his books there is no formula that will lay the evil spirits, if they once break loose. The arguments of his master, Proudhon, he cannot refute. He is a preacher of Communism, although he wants to stop half way. It is the interest of all owners of property, real or personal, to oppose to the utmost the spread of the influence of this demi-communist.

A BUSINESS MAN'S ANSWER.

FINALLY, let us examine Mr. George's theories from the standpoint of a New York business man.

His main proposition is that there exists an "unearned increment," which the State should take from land-owners. Thus he says on page 295 of his Social Problems:

"As society grows, so grows this value, which springs from and represents in tangible form what society as a whole contributes to production as distinguished from what is contributed by individual exertion. . . . Here is a fund belonging to society as a whole, from which, without the degradation of alms, private or public, provision can be made for the weak, the helpless, the aged; from which provision can be made for the common wants of all, as a matter of common right to each, etc."

But Mr. George nowhere proposes that society shall return the "unearned detriment."

If the State of New York should undertake to return all the money invested in lands in this State, with interest, and take the land in return, I doubt if it would make a good bargain. There is good farming land in Westchester County which does not now sell for as much as it cost to put up its stone fences.

If investors and builders do not come to a neighborhood, can the unfortunate speculator call upon the city to take his land at what he paid for it, with fair interest? If not, why should he be obliged to surrender the profit which he has acquired by his superior foresight?

Mr. George's friends evidently suppose that investors and builders do no work, in selecting sites, etc., but trust to luck. I recently asked a successful builder why he had purchased a certain site for some houses on the outskirts of Brooklyn. He said that he had counted that there were so many families living in houses beyond these lots, and that they had to pass them in order to go to the nearest stores; he counted the number of passers-by, considered their probable wealth, the chances of the neighborhood remaining a respectable one, etc., and finally decided that by purchasing those lots at such a price and erecting stores on them, the tenants of those stores could make certain profits, which would enable them to pay him a certain rent.

His calculations proved to be successful; the stores met a need of that neighborhood, and he secured a fair profit. Should now the City or the State come in and demand that profit from him, and distribute it among all the inhabitants, who had given no thought to the matter? If the State should do so, would this man be encouraged to select another site, and undergo the worry and excitement of erecting other buildings, which would so exactly meet a public demand?

If this principle is to be applied to profits made from investments in lands, why not to other investments? For example, a milliner foresees that taste is taking a certain direction, and that certain ornamentation will become fashionable, and manufactures and lays in a store of it; shall her entire profit be taken, when people come and wish to have that particular ornament, or shall only a certain per cent. be taken, and if so, what per cent.?

Or, if a man foresees that a certain place will have a rapid increase in population, and opens a store and transports a large stock of goods, and proceeds to meet the urgent demand, are his profits to be taken? Are they not due to the increase of the population, just as much as the increase in the land values of that place?

On page 82 of his "Social Problems," Mr. George makes the arguments against allowing profits to land-owners apply to owners of patent-rights and other personal property, although copyrights are not mentioned.

This is only another evidence that these theories are applicable to personal property, if they apply to real estate, and would put a stop to all speculative investments, which, in effect, only tend to preserve the fruits of the earth for a time when the people will have more need of them than at present.

But Mr. George makes no practical suggestion as to how this "unearned increment" is to be calculated. In what does the "earned increment" consist? Land in a desert, without inhabitants, has not much value; who settles a new country, except under the belief that it will be populated? Mr. George says, in the passage above cited, that society contributes its share in a "tangible form," but he does not say with which of our senses this is to be recognized. What a chance for corruption and favoritism would be opened by the attempt to carry out such a scheme!

But Mr. George does not condescend to give us any details as to how this shall be done; his only practical proposition is that all land shall be taxed up to its rental value, so that the owners shall surrender it to the State and the State is then to proceed to act the part of landlord. Let us suppose that all this has been done and the land in the city has been acquired by the municipality or State, which then proceeds to offer to lease it to individuals. Of course, in a city long leases would have to be given, especially if repairs or improvements are to be made by the tenants; large private corporations have found it advisable to give leases for twenty-one years with covenants for two or three renewals. What prices would the city be apt to realize? An intending bidder would, of course, wish to know how secure the title would be for which he was expected to give value; he would want to feel sure that the fee or term of years which he acquired would remain in him undisturbed. He would naturally inquire as to what had been the previous history of such purchasers of the fee or of leasehold interests from the city or from the State, and what would he find?

If he traced back the title to any piece of ground, he would come to a ground-brief from the Dutch authorities, or a grant from the British Crown; and back of that there was a purchase from the Indian inhabitants of this island. The Crown, which represented the State—the public of that day—received a valuable consideration for the conveyance; that money went into the public treasury, and an instrument was executed by the highest authority in the land, representing the people, conveying and assuring to the grantee the absolute title to the land to himself, and his heirs and assigns forever, with a covenant of warranty, by which the State agreed to defend the title to the lands so purchased at any time in future, when called upon to do so.

When the Revolution broke out, our State, in the Constitution of 1777, expressly pledged itself, by Article XXXVI., that "nothing in this Constitution contained shall be construed to affect any grant made by said king, or his predecessors," and that clause is in our Constitution to-day. It was, relying on this pledge, that the real-estate owners of this State risked their lives and their fortunes in favor of the Revolution, and enabled the State of New York to make so noble a record.

As to the upper part of the city, where the vacant lots lie, which Mr. George's friends so particularly abhor, the title to most of it was in the city up to a comparatively recent date; that formed part of the common lands of New York and Harlem. It was first leased for long terms to individuals for rents payable in a certain number of bushels of wheat, etc.—the book of leases can be seen in the Comptroller's office—and then later these rents were released on the payment of a lump sum to the city. Other parts of these commons were advertised and sold at public auction, some of it quite recently, and the money used to pay the city debts, build the acqueduct and wharves and lay out the Central Park. For these lands, the city executed full covenant and warranty deeds, conveying and assuring to the purchasers and to their successors forever, the absolute ownership to these lands. How can the people now demand that the acts of these public officers, elected by them, shall be nullified, and this land reclaimed, or any unfair burden placed upon it, violating thereby these solemn instruments?

The aqueduct, the Central Park, etc., were built with the money of these people: the city, the public, has received full value; it cannot recall these conveyances in the face of our constitutional prohibitions against violating the obligation of contracts or depriving individuals of their private property without compensation.

The policy which dictated these absolute conveyances was also wise. No one who knows what savage men and nature the early settlers had to contend with will doubt that this was necessary. Do we not know what hard work it took to make this island what it is? It was once a howling wilderness, where people lived only at the risk of their lives; all along the Bowery the farms were given up at one time for fear of the Indians, and later with difficulty could men be induced to live on them; you can read that in the records at the City Hall. Time and again were these houses plundered by the Indians.

But now, when that is all changed and forgotten, these men, whose ancestors remained comfortably in Europe, come here and demand it all, in the name of morality, justice, and heaven knows what, and say that land is as free as air, and sneer at these Dutch Indian-fighters.

Moreover, the natural difficulties which had to be overcome to make this island what it is, were great.

Let anyone look at the large map of this city, known as General Viele's map, which shows the natural aspect of this island, with its rocks, creeks, swamps and bays, and then let him estimate what it cost to make it the firm, level land that it is now. Who paid for these improvements? On the lots themselves their owners paid for the excavations, etc. And was it not, also, almost exclusively the owners of the lots fronting on the streets who paid the heavy assessments out of their own pockets for building even our streets, which we all use? and as to the share which was raised by taxation, do we not all know how little of that comes from personal property, but almost all from the land-owners, so that they have already practically paid for almost the whole of the city's public works.

Mr. George pretends to think that these even streets and level lots represent the natural condition of this island. He says, on page 81 of his "Social Poroblems," speaking of the settlement of this city: "If the Astors had all remained in Germany, or, if there had never been any Astors, the land of Manhattan Island would have been here all the same." True, the land would have been here; but, without the men who invested the fortunes which they brought with them, or made in business, in improving this land, Mr. George would have found this island as undesirable as any part of this rocky State which is still in a state of nature, and where land is to be had almost for the asking.

In fact, the right to no species of personal property has more guarantees under our Constitution and laws, or is entitled, on its own merits, to more consideration, than the right of property in land.

Considering all the facts, who would risk his money to purchase new titles, or take long leases, from such an Indian-giver as this State or City of New York? Who could tell how soon another demagogue would arise, and demand that the land should be sold over again? George repeats, most emphatically, Rousseau's arguments (which justified the anarchy of the French Revolution), that one generation cannot bind another.

In his "Irish Land Question," Mr. George says, on page 26: "It therefore follows, from the very fact of their existence, that the right of each one of the people of Ireland to an equal share in the land of Ireland, is equal and inalienable. . . . This right is irrefutable and indefeasible. . . . No law, no covenant, no agreement can bar it. One generation cannot stipulate away the rights of another generation. . . . If the whole people of Ireland were to unite in bargaining away their rights to the land, how could they justly bargain away the right of the child who the next moment is born?"

But, how is a generation to be reckoned? Need a child wait until it comes of age, if opportunity sooner offers? How about children who are under age at the time of this partition, and receive no share, or perhaps not what they consider an adequate share—can they demand a resale, or reletting, when they come of age?

In fact, Mr. George's scheme is nothing but repudiation

of the State and City's most solemn obligations. It would give a shock to public and to private credit, if any one supposed for a moment that there was any possibility of realizing such a scheme, compared to which any tampering with the currency would be child's play.

Nothing is heard, when Mr. George goes into practical politics, about any plan for compensation for "earned increment," but their only plan is to tax the owners of land, without reference to the improvements thereon. This shows how much Mr. George and his friends know of practical matters. This is only possible by taking the amount of money to be raised, and dividing it by the number of lots, and raising the quotient from each lot. For a lot can be valued for any purpose, in a city, only with reference to the improvements which are, or might be upon it; thus, assessors estimate the value of a vacant lot by considering what sort of a building could profitably be erected on it; then they estimate the rent of that building; then they deduct from the rent the interest on the capital required for the building, and other usual expenses of owners, and then they estimate upon how large a capital the remainder of the rent represents the interest, and that sum is taken as the value of the lot. A city lot has no value, except with reference to its actual or possible improvements, unless it be to pasture goats. If a building is already on the lot, and the assessors are told by Mr. George's party to value it without reference to the building, they can do so only by considering the value of some imaginary building on the lot; that constitutes the selling value of a lot.

The only approach to a practical plan of the "Progressive Democracy" is, therefore, simply silly and impossible, and the only practical effect would be to tax Vanderbilt's palace no more than a row of houses on Varick street, or a cabbage-garden in the Twenty-fourth Ward.

But, supposing that this scheme could, in some way, be carried out, so as to compel all owners to build on their vacant lands at once, what would be the result? What land is there now which is not built upon? It is land which is so situated that the owners believe that in future there will be greater need for it by the public for other purposes than those for which the people would now use it, and that the expense of preparing it for this temporary use would exceed the returns. If an owner thinks that his lot will soon be in demand, as a factory or warehouse, he will not put up a tenement house on it, because, although he might raise the necessary money by a mortgage, yet, that debt would prevent him subsequently raising the amount necessary to tear down the tenement house and build the factory, when the latter became more important for the wants of the people. The judgment of real-estate owners on these points can generally be trusted; they have every interest in getting an income from their land; if it lies in a good situation, and is not built upon, the owner will be continually called upon by agents, suggesting various purposes to which it could be put. To suppose that our public salaried officials would exhibit an equal zeal or judgment in these matters, is absurd.

If Mr. George and his friends are so improvident as not to see that the only practical measures which they propose will inevitably fail to carry out their schemes for the present, need we wonder that they are unable to look far enough into the past and future, and, consequently, fail to appreciate the disastrous consequences which their theories would have, if put into practice, upon the future material and moral welfare of our country, by destroying all the humanizing influences which cluster around the ownership of a home, by terminating the inducements which are necessary, even now, to lead men to make the great sacrifices necessary to make habitable a new country in the Great West, or to extend our Eastern cities, and finally, by teaching men to violate, for the sake of present material comfort, the most solemn obligations, and to disregard the commandments, "Thou shalt not covet," and "Thou shalt not steal?"

A WORKINGMAN'S ANSWER.

ON Saturday I received a note from the gentleman who at our meeting on last Monday most zealously sustained Mr. George's theories, in which he stated that I had at that time not represented the workingmen's side of the question, and that consequently my argument was undemocratic. I considered that I had answered Mr. George when I had shown that his proposal was unjust.

However, without admitting that the Democratic party is exclusively the party of the workingmen, I intend this evening to consider Mr. George's candidacy from the stand-point of a workingman, and to ascertain for what reasons they ought to support him.—I will assume that the justice of his propositions is proven, and that the only question is one of expediency, namely, what the workingmen would gain if his theories as announced in his platform were put into practice.

The best expression of the present wishes of the workingmen that I know of, is to be found in the constitutions of the various trades unions. One of the most prominent unions is Typographical Union No. 6; § 3 of its Constitution reads : " The objects of this union shall be the maintenance of a fair rate of wages, the encouragement of good workingmen, and the employment of every means which may tend to the elevation of printers in social life." The Constitution of the Cigar Makers Union begins : " Whereas it is the duty of every worker to unite with his fellow worker to secure a fair compensation for his labor ; to elevate the condition of the lowest paid worker to the standard of the highest ; to provide for the sick members and bury the dead."

The Furniture Workers Union has the following objects:

> a) The maintenance and increase of wages. b) The reduction of the hours of labor. c) The assistance during strikes and lockouts. d) The assistance while unemployed. e) The assistance during sickness. f) The assistance in case of death. g) The assistance in case of loss of tools. h) The rendering of legal assistance in claims against employers. i) The instruction by lectures.

The Cigar Makers International Union of America is formed to improve themselves : " By prevailing upon the Legislature to secure first the prohibition of child labor under 14 years of age ; the establishment of a normal day's labor to consist of not more than 8 hours per day for all classes ; the abolition of the truck system, tenement house cigar manufacture, and the system of letting out by contract the convict labor in prisons and reformatory institutions ; the legalization of trade unions and the establishment of bureaus of labor statistics."

To these objects in the main, no fair-minded citizen can object ; let us see what Mr. George will do towards their realization.

The practical change proposed in his platform is to tax real estate without reference to the improvements, so that no one could afford to hold unimproved land but would be compelled to build immediately. Without stopping now to consider the practicability of this scheme, let us assume that it has been done, and that a large number of houses suited for dwellings and manufactures and offices have been built, so as to reduce rents throughout the city very materially, or even to a mere nominal sum. What advantage would that be to the workingmen ?

I am an employee of a large corporation ; if the rent of its various offices were reduced or entirely abolished, my pay would in no way be increased,—very possibly I might never hear of it ; I believe the men employed in any business in this city would say the same thing.

But if the rent of my apartment were reduced very materially, it would benefit me, if it was done in my case alone; but if it were done throughout the city, very soon my employers would say : "We hear you no longer pay rent; that is probably so much of your salary ; we intend to reduce your salary that much, and if you are not satisfied, we can now get a man of equal ability for that pay, as other men in your branch have also to pay no rents." Even if all employers did not do this at once, some would certainly begin it, and then the others would be forced to follow suit, or be undersold or driven out of the business. I believe the men employed in any trade or manufacture in this city would say that this would surely happen. Morover, where would the money come from with which these houses are to be built ? Would it not be taken out of the trades and manufactures, where it is now invested, because it receives a larger return, and would not all these other trades and manufactures, and the men employed therein suffer ?

Or if the large amount of money which it is expected will be immediately raised by taxation were wisely expended for beneficent public purposes, and heat and light were furnished without charge to all citizens, would not employees soon hear similar remarks about the saving which they were now making in the matter of light and fuel, and would not one employer after the other make a consequent reduction in wages, as stated above in the case if rents were reduced ?

Would the workingmen not be in exactly the position in which they are to-day? Would not this money expected for these public benefits also attract workingmen from other cities, and so leave this same old contest between labor and capital? Would there not be the same necessity for the Declaration of the Principles of the Knights of Labor of North America, beginning : " The alarming development and aggression of aggregated wealth, which, unless checked, will inevitably lead to the pauperization and hopeless degradation of the toiling masses, render it imperative, if we desire to enjoy the blessings of life, that a check should be placed upon its power and upon unjust accumulation, and a system adopted which will secure to the laborer the fruits of his toil " ?

Would not the fight against over-work, child-labor, the truck-system, and all the acknowledged evils of the *laissez-faire* system have to be begun again, just where they are now ?

I submit therefore that this movement, as defined in their platform, can not accomplish the ends which workingmen desire and which would really benefit them; the amount of their pay would continue to be regulated by the most unscrupulous and hard-hearted man among the class of their employers.

But I believe that this movement will do more than this; I believe that it will very seriously injure the real interests of the workingmen and indefinitely postpone the realization of all practical plans for the improvement of their condition. In the first place, they are wasting their energies in electing an administrative officer, instead of trying to secure representatives in the legislature, who would secure the changes on our statute book, necessitated by our transition from a purely agricultural state to one having large manufacturing interests. No one knows what ought to be proposed in this matter so well as the workingmen themselves and unless they send representatives, their just demands will not be attended to. The same thing applies to our local legislature, the Board of Aldermen; the workingmen have announced their intention of not paying attention to these offices, but of concentrating their efforts on the Mayor. It is already evident that both Aldermen and Assemblymen are to be of the same class as in former years; that they will be the tools of politicians and corporations, as in former years; and that the workingmen will get as much benefit, as they have got in former years. But this is not all the mischief: the demands which the workingmen make for shorter hours, etc., can be conceded to them only at a certain loss and sacrifice on the part of other classes of the community. Hitherto their demands have met generally with fair popular support; for instance the early closing movement. But let the workingmen adhere to Mr. George's theories and they will antagonize a very large class of the people of this State, and drive them to unite with the employers, so that the demands of the workingmen will meet with a very different reception, after a few campaigns such as this promises to be.

That Mr. George's theories are not actually going to be put into practice, every practical man knows; "the statesmanship of the plough," which, as Governor Seymour said, guides this country, forbids it; the whole movement is too much against the American traditions; the Churches will all be against it; the influence which a combination of employers and real estate owners would bring to bear, if once aroused, with all their friends, would simply overwhelm the trades-unions. Moreover, Mr. George's theories, as soon as they are brought to light and their practical application considered, will cause so many new theorists to spring up with equally visionary plans, who will oppose each other, so that all will cease to have attractions for any large number of citizens sufficiently strong to hold them together.

I do not therefore think that, admitting that the argument which I first advanced this evening were false, and that the workingmen could realize benefits from this plan, that there is the remotest prospect of its being put into operation. But I do think that it will immediately excite hostility among a very large and important class and that the real reforms needed by workingmen will thereby be delayed.

The experience of Europe during the last century shows the certain futility of this movement. The first man to undertake to put these theories into practice was Babœuf, at the close of the first French Revolution ; Proudhon was the first to undertake to justify it, and Considerant (in 1837), a pupil of Fourier, modified the doctrine so that it should only apply to land, and not to personal property.

How closely Mr. George has followed these authors a few citations, showing the main points of their theories, will demonstrate.

To begin with the title page of Mr. George's first book, which reads : "Progress and Poverty : an Inquiry into the cause of industrial depressions, *and of increase of want with increase of wealth*"; the article cited in note A, of Mr. Considerant's Socialism (published in 1849) is entitled : "Of the causes of the increase of misery in proportion to the development of riches."—This article states the proposition as follows : "If there is a social phenomenon worthy of attention, it is certainly that of the increase of misery among the laboring classes in proportion to the progress of general wealth, and that other phenomenon not less extraordinary and always accompanying the latter, of this misery existing most intensely among the most industrious and free nations, like England, France etc."

Mr. George says in his Progress and Poverty, p. 7 : "It is at last becoming evident that the enormous increase in productive power has no tendency to extirpate poverty. It is in the older and richer sections of the Union that pauperism and distress among the working classes are becoming most painfully apparent." (p. 9.)

Mr. Considerant impressively says: "The Sphinx is the people; the terrible enigma is the problem of the times." Mr. George says on yage 9: "It is the riddle which the Sphinx of fate puts to our civilization, and which not to answer is to be destroyed."

In Considerant's other work, entitled "Destinée Sociale" (1837) he says on page 250: "It is then proved by facts that the proletariat and pauperism increase in epochs of civilization with population and more rapidly than it, and as the direct cause of the growing progress of industry."—He repeats the same statement in various forms, as often as Mr. George does.—We see therefore that the problem which these two writers propose, is the same.

As to the remedy, they also agree and Mr. Considerant says, in his work of 1837: "The whole land must be cultivated as the land of one man." In the work of Mr. Considerant entitled "Socialism" he says on page 107; "Rent of land is a feudal privilege which ought to go to rejoin its elder brethren in the great ditch of justice of the Nations and Revolutions.... There are among Socialists those who would derange nothing in society; who do not call us to live in common, to abandon that which we have, to change our manner of life for something we know not what .. Suppose that these socialists should come to power and this should be then law."

Mr. George says on page 364 of Progress and Poverty: "It is not necessary to confiscate land; it is only necessary to confiscate rent."

Mr. Considerant does not enter to any extent into an attempt to show the justice of this appropriation of land by the public; so Mr. George has to take up Proudhon, for this part of the argument, and repeats in various forms the latters three arguments.

Firstly Mr. Proudhon says in his book on Property (I cite from the translation published by Tucker, Princeton, Mass..

1876): "How can the supplies of nature, the wealth created by Providence, become private property? We want to know by what right man has appropriated wealth which he did not create, and which nature gave to him gratuitously? Who made the land? God. Then proprietor, retire." (p. 89). Mr. George says in Social Problems (p. 278): "What more preposterous than the treatment of land as individual property... It is the creation of God."

Proudhon's second point is that universal consent gives no justification to property, he says (p. 311 in Theorie de l'Import): "The earth furnishes to man the material, tools and force.—Labor puts force in motion.—Labor alone is productive. Now to recognize the right of territorial property is to give up labor, since it is to relinquish the means of labor." Mr. George says in the chapter on "Injustice of Private Property in Land," in Progress and Poverty: "land on which and from which all must live. The recognition of private individual proprietorship of land is the denial of the natural rights of other individuals. For as labor can not produce without the use of land, the denial of the equal right to the use of land is necessarily the denial of the right of labor to its produce."

Proudhon's third argument is that "proscription (or long possession) gives no title to property; it is not based on a just title; past error is not binding on the future," p. 89.

Mr. George says on 307 of Progress and Poverty; "Consider for a moment the utter absurdity of the titles, by which we permit it to be passed from John Doe to Richard Roe .. Everywhere not to a right which obliges, but to a force which compels, and when a title rests but on force, no complaint can be made when force annuls it."

Proudhon's conclusion is: "The earth cannot be appropriated," (p. 73 of French edition). — Mr. George says: "There is on earth no power which can rightfully make a grant of exclusive ownership of land," (p. 304 of Progress and Poverty).

Proudhon then abuses owners, for example, citing a verse which shows how first comes the contractors share, then the laborers, then the capitalists and then: "I am the proprietor. I take the whole," (p. 189).—Mr. George says in Protection and Free Trade: "And the robber that takes all that is left is private property in land," (p. 285).—The number of these comparisons might be increased very largely. Finally, in his picture of the results, Mr. George returns to Considerant, and insists with him upon the great advantages to individuals arising from this cooperation and common ownership of all living in the commune, and as the picture of a Utopia one is as beautiful as the other. We see therefore that as to his title, problem, its solution, the remedy of the evil and the result Mr. George has followed Considerant, and as to the justification of the remedy Proudhon.—Unfortunately Proudhon proves too much ; for as I showed in my former paper, if Mr. George has demonstrated that there should be no private property in land, he has also demonstrated this as to personal property.— Proudhon proclaimed this, and it was the chief difference between him and Considerant.

If we delay for a moment to call in mind the resemblances which I have pointed out to Proudhon and Considerant,— and they can be greatly increased if any one will take the trouble so to do, by comparing these books in the Astor Library,—can we accept the generally received theory as to George's intellectual capacity or of his extraordinary devotion to humanity, or even of his phenomenal honesty ? What must we think of those men who have compared his doctrines to those of Christ ? Is it not an insult to our intelligence to dish up these warmed-up meats from which Europe has long ago turned away in disgust, as the heaven-born manna which alone can preserve the New World ? If the ghosts of Messieurs Proudhon and Considerant were allowed to sit on the stage at one of Mr. George's meetings, would not his remarks be often interrupted by their indignant chestnut-bells?

But to resume: What success had this theory in France? Babœuf's rude announcement of it was the closing episode of the first French Revolution and made Napoleon I. possible; the fear of it sustained the Restoration and the July Monarchy; Proudhon and Considerant were in the Assemblée of the 1848 Republic, and Considerant then published his socialism above cited, and announced that in three years the social-democratic republic would be in force; in far less time the second Empire was established, as necessary for the preservation of order.

Since then, these theories have in Europe passed from the stage of practical politics and are only referred to by historians as showing the steps by which modern socialism, as advocated by Karl Marx and Lasalle arose. It is the oblivion to which these older radical thorists have been consigned by the modern communists themselves, which induced the French bourgeoisie to support the present Republic. If therefore this seed of dragons' teeth could not sprout in France and has now rotted in the ground, we need not fear that it will bear fruit in this much more uncongenial clime. Nor need we fear that the people will accept a despotism in order to escape it; the true proportions of this movement will be known soon enough. But we must fear that this movement will excite hostility against the workingmen among a large class of our well-to-do population, especially in our cities, and also that it will induce this class to submit with excessive patience to the increasing growth of the power of the monopolists and politicians, for fear that any change in our old-fashioned countrified government might be for the worse.

But this revival of worn-out Old-World theories is also injurious to the workingmen, in turning them from the pursuit of the theories of Lasalle and Karl Marx, many of which, all must recognize, have a certain amount of justice. Those writers recognize the necessity of a historical development and aim at improving the workingmen's condition by introducing factory regulations, shorter hours, etc., as our trades-unions' circulars above cited demanded. To turn back the hands of the clock for forty years and take up these impracticable chimeras, means an injury to the real welfare of the workingmen, and of our whole people, which it is difficult to under-estimate.

The dread which those theories excited in France, so as to drive men to accept the First and Second Empire, may also be a warning to us of the effect which even a moderate success of this movement at the polls, would have upon capital invested in this City and State. I fear that a vote of even 20,000 will be sufficient to give a check to our industries, which are just now reviving under the influence of general prosperity; failing trade and closing factories will be in proportion to the success of this movement, and the only real change in the condition of the working men.

There is another benefit which we derive from tracing Mr. George's ideas to their source: When we see how many of his theories he has evidently taken from Considerant, who advocated the co-operative communes with all land in common, we are able to understand many suggestions of Mr. George, as being part of a more or less definite intention of realizing some such scheme, and which ideas appear disconnected and unintelligible, if we consider solely his intentions of abolishing rent as his one object, with which he would be satisfied.

Thus, I was surprised to find Mr. George advocating the increase of the power of our Board of Aldermen. He says, in the interview published in the *Sun* of October 3: "New York (city) should have one legislative body that in local affairs would have sovereign power." There was no demand for this in the platform, nor so far as I know have the workingmen demanded it ; the whole tendency of legislation has been to deprive this Board of power ; Mr. George does not suggest any manner of improving its character,—but only wants it to have " sovereign power."—Without stopping to dwell on the fact that if Mr. George were a real Democrat he would not admit that any government was " sovereign " over the people, I think the explanation for this strange demand is that it is an essential part of Considerant's theory of the co-operative commune. This absolute local government is necessary for any scheme of communism; if all are to enjoy equally, all must work equally, and this requires strict supervision. It was the demand of the Paris communists; the beautiful Utopia that makes Mr. George's book so attractive cannot be realized without it. No matter how much he may strive to keep it in the back-ground, he cannot hide the cloven hoof. Thus he says on page 296 of Social Questions, that " society may pass into a co-operative association," and on page 410 of Progress and Poverty : " Government would change its character, and would become the administration of a great co-operative society. It would become merely the agency by which the common property was administered for the common benefit." This is only Considerant's communal government ; how much official machinery would be necessary in New York to realize Mr. George's plans, as set out for example, on page 410 of Progress and Poverty: " This revenue arising from the common property could be applied to common benefit, as were the revenues of Sparta. We might not establish public tables—they would become unnecessary ; but we could establish public baths, museums, libraries, gardens, lecture rooms, music and dancing halls, theatres, universities, technical schools, shooting galleries, play-grounds, gymnasiums, etc." Society attempts some of these things now ; how does it realize them ? Had we not better get our present undertakings in good working order, before starting out on such unlimited extensions of the system ?

Moreover, this demand for one sovereign local government, over the million and a half of people of this city, and which is absolutely necessary for the realization of half of Mr. George's schemes, presents the chief objection to all that is hopeful in the modern labor movement. That movement recognizes the necessity of trades unions, that they have come to stay, that in their proper development and participation in public affairs lies great promise for the welfare not only of the workingmen, but of the State; and that these trade organizations should be entrusted with powers and duties and form part of our body politic, as the geographical divisions called States and Counties made up the Union when we were purely an agricultural community.

Now these trades unions have as much need for the democratic doctrine of wheels within wheels, and as little need for a sovereign local government over them, as the States have for a sovereign and therefore unlimited national government (see Mr. Bancroft's Plea for the Constitution,* and this radical difference between trades unionists and socialists has long been instinctively recognized in labor circles, and the contest between the two has been for years going on with varying success; see the following citation on page 602 of the Third Annual Report of the Bureau of Labor Statistics of New York: "To confound the trade union movement with the political movement of the Socialists is a thorough mistake, the difference being that while the trades unions are organized only for the purpose of protection for their labor, adapting themselves at all times to circumstances and conditions as well as to the surroundings, and being largely influenced thereby, the socialistic movement aims at the entire reconstruction of society upon their principles, is satisfied with nothing

---

* See also: "Tendencies of the Republican Party," published by this Club

less, ignores all possible reasonable objections, and disparages trade organizations, recognizing them only as obstacles in their path of progress."

Now, it is plain that Mr. George with his demand for a sovereign, *i. e.* unlimited local government belongs to the communist-socialistic school, — as every faithful desciple of Proudhon and Considerant should ; and it is also for this reason that I believe that workingmen, who believe in trades unions, should oppose Mr. George.

Trades unions have no place in Mr. George's schemes ; according to the index, they are not mentioned in Progress and Poverty ; in Protection and Free Trade they are referred to three times,—two of which are bare mentions, and the third (on pages 322 and 323) is as follows : " Something can be done in this way for those within such organizations; but it is after all very little .... This, those who are inclined to put faith in the power of trades-unionism are beginning to see, aud the logic of events must more and more lead them to see."—Mr. George therefore has no faith in trades-unions.—Are the skilled workingmen then going to allow their organizations to be used for this man's election ? Have they not had enough experience with theorists, politicians aud demagogues (often in the pay of employers) who did not believe in their unions ? Among his supporters are found men whose interests are identified with bodies which have always opposed trades unions. *A vote for Henry George is a vote against the Trades Unions.*

On the other hand, if the workingmen, as members of their trades-unions, would make a demand on the Democratic Party for recognition of their representatives in the party's councils, they would before long, I am convinced, receive due attention, and be able to have an influence on legislation and choice of officers proportionate to the importance of their organizations. The demands of these unions for recognition by the State, and for a certain amount of autonomy in their internal affairs, is justified by all the Democratic Fathers in their advocacy of State Rights.

Or else the workingmen could in local matters go into politics by themselves and seek to gain the practical objects which their constitutions have so long demanded; for this they should elect members of the Legislature, instead of having their Central Committee, as it has to-day done, prohibit the organizations to indorse or put forward candidates. There is where the source of evil lies; in the reckless bad laws which the Legislatures pass. But if the workingmen say they cannot elect Assemblymen, because they are divided into so many districts that their strength is wasted, then they should strive to abolish this unnatural division into geographical election districts. But it is worse than useless for workingmen to try to put these wild theorists who can only alarm men of property into administrative offices.*

It is the old story of that which happened in Rome, where the wild pleas for the division of land by the Gracchi drove the Romans to accept a plutocracy and finally the Cæsars. As above mentioned, it was the similar demand for common land, which led to the overthrow of the first and second French Republics. Can we not profit by their experience?

Can we not do these things better in America?

This, I think, will be the turning point in American history. No republic has ever yet passed from the condition of an agricultural community to that of a state with large cities, without being plagued by demagogues—especially

---

* Under the Consolidation Act of 1882 the men who assess land for taxation, are sworn to value improved and unimproved land equally at its selling value. What selling value has city property if the actual or possible improvements are not considered?

those who demanded a division of land—until refuge was taken in a depotism.

If we can introduce those trade organizations in a peaceable and orderly manner into our body politic—a feat which no state has yet accomplished—and satisfy their just demands, I believe that we would have a state, which might realize some of Considerant's beautiful aspirations, here in America, although his French methods are impracticable. America must find its own way. Let us remember what Emerson said:

"We live in a new and exceptional age. America is another name for Opportunity. Our whole history appears like a last effort of the Divine Providence in behalf of the human race."

Progress and Justice; or, The Work for Federalism.

Bismarck is reported to have said: "There was some justification for Parisian communism." May it not then be worth while for us to inquire whether there is not some grievance, which caused over sixty thousand of our fellow citizens at the last election to vote for the representative of such wild theories as those of Henry George, evidently merely as an indignant protest against the existing order of things, in this "land of the free and home of the brave?" Anyone who looks back upon the last few years and sees how rapidly this discontent has spread and organized for political action, must realize that it is not a matter which this generation can afford to disregard. Especially is it incumbent upon anyone who may believe in the principles set forth in my "Trade Organizations in Politics," to consider whether in the light of recent occurences its theories, favoring the development of trade, business and professional organizations must not be considered as dangerous, at this time and in our country.

I believe, however, that if we will patiently examine this workingmen's movement, we will find in it, among much that is reprehensible, many signs of promise, and that we will realize that the great question is how to encourage the latter and repress the former, and that by a courageous and charitable spirit the development of this movement may be so guided as to produce the greatest benefits, not only to the workingmen, but to society at large.

In the first place, no one need assume that this movement is to grow indefinitely; the differences of interest which exist between the skilled and unskilled workingmen are already making themselves felt in the contests between the old trade unionists and the Knights of Labor. The latter require a strong centralized organization, governing all laborers engaged in occupations requiring little or no skill, so as to keep the great army of unskilled labor from migrating to any section where a strike may exist, and taking up the employment which the strikers have dropped; to render a strike of such laborers successful, the unemployed men of the whole country must be controlled. Skilled workingmen, on the other hand, need fear only the competition of men who have devoted years to prepare themselves for the trade; they therefore have but little dread of competition from the great mass of day laborers. The unskilled workingmen are consequently called upon to contribute for the success of strikes in all parts of the country, as they can only hope to improve their own condition by raising that of all other unskilled laborers. The carpenters or engineers, on the other hand, while they have a much more direct interest in the success of a strike in their own trade in any part of the country, have but little concern as to the condition of hod carriers or freight handlers.

The disputes in the United Labor Party are therefore unavoidale and certain to increase, so that there is no cause for excessive alarm. Moreover, as any communistic movement nears apparent success, it is actually approaching destruction; for the reason that then its leaders must unfold their plans, how their theories are to be practically realized, and there is none that will obtain the approval of workingmen. Common enjoyment of the earth's prod ucts can exist only with their common production; this common production can be made fair only by the strictest government supervision, and this is exactly what communists object to. The International in Europe flourished there but recently; it was so successful that its members at last began discussing what they would do when Government was actually in their hands; that discussion broke up their organization and it is now no longer heard of.

The study of history shows also that attempts to introduce equality of property have all failed, and anyone who appreciates the stability of legal institutions, and their slow change even among distantly related races and in different climes, will feel sure that we are not at the utmost approaching anything except temporary disorders.

But this danger is one sufficiently serious to demand the most careful consideration of all who feel an interest in the country's welfare. Is it not possible to discover and remove the cause of this discontent, ere it breaks out in violence? That the condition of masses of our fellow beings in our great American cities is most wretched is undeniable. Their condition can not be ascertained by comparing their food or wages with that of European workmen. Our climate is so exhilarating and exhausting, the cold and heat are so extreme, that the comforts required to make life here endurable much exceed those needed in Europe. No one acquainted with New York City in summer will deny that for about three months the condition of operatives, who spend their days in crowded factories and their nights in tenement houses, is one which entails long and severe physical suffering, and which renders mental and moral improvement extremely difficult; in the raw cold of our winter days and nights, they are again exposed to severe strains upon their constitutions, by which many sicken or have their lives shortened.

The progress of science has led to the discovery of many means by which articles may be manufactured more cheaply or with more attractive appearance, than heretofore; but at the expense of the health of the operatives, although the evil effects of their occupation are often not immediately apparent.

In short, no one can pretend that the condition of the working classes in our great cities is a satisfactory one. But the aggravation of this condition consists in its being, as a rule, permanent. Our city is full of rich men, who were workingmen in their youth, and yet if you ask them whether they could begin to-day as a workingman and repeat their success, they would tell you that it could not be done. No one has set forth the evils suffered by workingmen and the present hopelessness of their fate, more eloquently than Mr. George, and in my opinion his description is not overdrawn as to our large cities. His explanation is false and his remedy is vain, as I have tried, to show. Is there another explanation of this evil, and is there another remedy?

I know that Mr. Mill is supposed to have settled this question by the mysterious theories of "supply and demand," "competition," etc., and to have shown that the actual condition is the best possible and that legislation can produce no real improvement; but there are some considerations which this pessimistic school does not sufficiently consider.

In my opinion anyone who makes inquiries among workingmen and employers in our cities will find tha Thornton in his work on "Labor," by which he forced Mr. Mill to confess the inadequacy of the famed wage-fund theory, is correct when he says (p. 101): "What really does, within certain impassable limits, regulate wages, is commonly, when the employed are content to remain passive, the combination of the employers; and when these have (as they in practice do far more and far oftener than they get credit for) fixed upon a higher rate than they need have done, they can, of course, lower it if they please. . . . Now, among keenly competing employers, there are never wanting some who are willing to reduce wages so much as possible. . . . But scarcely more true is it of Ireland, or of India, than of England, that whatever has, at any time, been the minimum of subsistence—supposed to be sufficient to enable laborers to go on living as they had been accustomed to live—that some minimum has been the measure of the price of labor. Whenever and wherever masters have had the framing of the scale of wages, this has been the basis of their calculations (p. 147). . . . Instead of suffering the rate of wages to be settled naturally by competition, they endeavor by combination to settle it arbitrarily (p. 80). But it is only very rarely, and when labor is at once very scarce and in very great request, that masters are tempted to compete with each other. At all other times they are in the habit of combining, instead of competing, and it is their combination which then determines the price of labor, and determines it arbitrarily. . . . Combined masters really possess—whether they choose to exercise or not—almost absolute power of control over the wages of uncombined workmen. . . . Thus in a normal state of things, . . . the price of labor is determined not by supply and demand, which never determined the price of anything, nor yet generally by competition, which generally determines the price of everything else, but by combination among the masters" (pp. 83-85). Mr. Mill, in his reply to Mr. Thornton, in the 'Fortnightly Review," in effect admitted the justice of the latter's criticism, to the considerable dismay of his own scholars. He says, on page 690: "In this higgling, the laborer in an isolated condition, unable to hold out even against a single employer—much more against the tacit combination of employers—will, as a rule, find his wages kept down at the lower limit."

Anyone who will take the trouble to inquire in actual life, or to consult the Report of the Bureau of Labor Statistics for 1886, will find that, in this State and in this time, what Adam Smith said is true: "Masters are always and everywhere in a sort of tacit but uniform combination not to raise wages above their actual rate."

Furthermore, it appears to be true what Cairnes said, in his "Leading Principles of Political Economy": "What we find in effect is not a whole population competing indiscriminately for all occupations, but a series of industrial layers, superposed on one another, within each of which the various candidates for employment possess a real and effective power of selection, while those occupying the several strata are for all purposes of effective competition practically isolated from one another" (p. 64).

Sir John Lubbock, in a recent article on the early closing movement in "Good Words," said: "Happily, I may say this is no question between shopkeepers and their assistants. There is no such difference. I believe the shopkeepers are almost as anxious to close as the assistants themselves. Perhaps, then, it may be said, why not leave the matter in their hands? Because in almost every case the arrangements for early closing have been rendered nugatory by the action of some very small minority among the shopkeepers. Over and over again the shopkeepers in a given district have been anxious to close, and have all agreed to do so with, perhaps, a single exception. But that single exception is fatal. One after another the rest gradually open again, the whole thing breaks down, and thus a small minority tyrannize over the rest."

Bearing in mind these three propositions, namely, that the rate of wages in every trade is mainly determined by an open or secret combination of the employers, and that the most unscrupulous employer in any trade can force other employers to be equally oppressive to their employees, under penalty of being driven out of the business, and that workingmen in the trades requiring any training are not able to go at will from one trade to another—is it true that legislation ought and can do nothing towards permanently improving the condition of the workingmen? Firstly, as to the "ought," the answer of Mr. Mill and his followers is plain. Cairnes, in his work above cited, says: " I am unaware of any rule of justice applicable to the problem of distributing the produce of industry" (p. 263). Thornton says in his book " On Labor": "Either side is clearly at liberty to put forward whatever claim it pleases. The only question is whether it is strong enough to enforce its claim" (p. 301). Professor Sumner says in his "What Social Classes Owe One Another": "Society does not need any care or supervision (p. 119). . . . There is no injunction, no 'ought' in political economy at all" (p. 156).

To counterbalance these opinions of the Manchester school, I would refer to the writings of the modern German political economists, who constitute the so-called Professorial-Socialist school. Thus, Schmoller says in his "Ueber einige Grundfragen" (p. 159): "Law and humanity must not be banished even from political economy;" and on page 90: " A great part of this injustice arises because, in times of new economical development, morality and law are at first ineffectual against the actual power of the rich." These sentiments are re-echoed by all the energetic writers of this school, and it is their theories which are being followed out in the present successful German legislation for the regeneration of the working classes. As Rae says of this school, in his "Contemporary Socialism" (p. 202): "They said it was vain for the Manchester party to deny that a social question existed, and to maintain that the working classes were as well off as it was practical for economical arrangements to make them. They declared there was much truth in the charges which socialists were bringing against the existing order of things, and that there was a decided call upon all the powers of society—and, among others, especially upon the State—to intervene with some remedial measures."

Even the writers of the Manchester school—while their official programme denies the propriety of any interference with individuals in economical matters—let fall many expressions entirely inconsistent with this claim. Thus, Mr. Mill says in the article in the "Fortnightly Review," for May, 1869, above cited: "Every opinion as to the relative rights of laborers and employers involves, expressly or tacitly, some theory of justice, and it cannot be indifferent to know what theory" (p. 506). The Report of the English Labor Law Commissioners, in 1867 (see "Davis' Labor Laws"), contains the following passage: "All that, as it appears to us, the law has to do, *over and above any protection that may be required for classes unable to protect themselves*, such as women and children, is to secure a fair field for the unrestricted exercise of industrial competition." Finally, even Professor Sumner, in the same book from which the heartless principles above cited were taken, says: "The safety of workmen from machinery, the ventilation and sanitary arrangements required by factories, the special precautions of certain processes, the hours of labor of women and children, the limits of age for employed children,

Sunday work, hours of labor—these, and other like matters, ought to be controlled by the men (workingmen) themselves, through their organizations."

Surely, this programme of practical reforms ought to be sufficient for the present to satisfy even ardent reformers; but is it not plainly inconsistent with the *laissez-faire* doctrines, above cited, of the same eminent professor, as well as with the teachings concerning personal liberty of the founders of this school? The late Mr. Jevons, in his work entitled "The State in Relation to Labor," confesses that this main doctrine of the Manchester school is a failure; he says: " Evidently there must be cases where it is incumbent on one citizen to guard against the danger to other citizens. But even in the extreme case of the adult man, experience unquestionably shows that men from mere thoughtlessness or ignorance incur grave injuries to health or limb which very little pressure from the Legislature could avert with benefit to all parties" (p. 5). " It is no doubt a gross interference with that metaphysical entity, the liberty of the subject, to prevent a man from working with phosphorus as he pleases; but if it can be shown by unquestionable statistics and the unimpeachable evidence of scientific men that such working with phosphorus leads to a dreadful disease, easily preventable by a small change of procedure, then I hold that the Legislature is *prima facie* justified in obliging the man to make this small change. The liberty of the subject is only the means towards an end" (p. 12.) And this eminent writer finally confesses: " The question may well arise indeed, whether, according to the doctrine here upheld, there is really any place at all for rules and general propositions" (p. 17).

This confession of failure appears to be the final conclusion to which the Manchester school has come; and yet there must be some general principles by which all these particular cases are to be governed; there must remain a science of legislation on economic matters.

The fault which, as it seems to me, has led to the decay of the Manchester school, is its indifference to the exercise of the principles of justice between classes or groups of men, or between the State and such classes or groups. Thus, Professor Sumner says, on p. 160 of his above cited work: "The relations of sympathy and sentiment are essentially limited to two persons only, and they cannot be made a basis for the relations of groups of persons, or for discussion by any third party." But if it is my duty as an individual not to trample on but to show compassion to another individual, who may be suffering, is it not also my duty to show compassion and not to trample upon a number of individuals or class? And is it not equally my duty when acting not individually, but with a number of others or in a class, to show the same spirit and not to trample upon another individual or class? All classes combined, or the State, owe sympathy to an individual, as evidenced by public charitable institutions, courts of justice, etc.; should not the same spirit be shown to a number of individuals, or to a class? The State compels one individual to show sympathy to another; why may it not insist on a number of individuals or a class showing sympathy to an individual, or to a number of individuals or class? Why should it allow one class to destroy another physically, morally and spiritually, when it does not permit one individual so to destroy another? Is not the former, if anything, the greater wrong?

The position of the Manchester school differs in no way from that of the first man who said: "Am I my brother's keeper?" Christianity in making the love of neighbor, as illustrated by the parable of the Good Samaritan, its second great commandment, says that we are.

As I have tried to show in my paper on Federalism, the

root of law is in this God-given feeling of sympathy, and that the spirit which pervades it is love.

Sir Matthew Hale said: "Christianity is parcel of the law of England."

If, therefore, we admit that the law can enforce the exercise of sympathy between individuals, it must also, in my opinion, be able to enforce such sympathy between classes.

The great change which is now occurring in this country, as it is being filled up, is the formation of classes of men who do not, as formerly, go from one occupation to another, but who remain for life in the same pursuit of a living. In our political economy we must therefore begin with the injunction in the song of the herald-angels: "Peace on earth, good-will amongst men;" or, as St. Paul expands it in Epistle to the Colossians, Ch. III., v. 2: "Where there is neither Greek nor Jew, circumcision, nor uncircumcision, Barbarian, Scythian, bond nor free; but Christ is all, and in all."

We should cast off the name of Christians if we believe that in our business life, which comprises, probably, the greater part of our energies, mutual consideration and justice are to have no place.

Or, on merely patriotic grounds, if we assume that a State is a being created to develop particularly certain faculties, or realize certain ideals, must we not be willing to limit our absolute liberty, in order to realize these ideals? How could society otherwise have been formed? In the words of Cobbett: "There never yet was, and never will be, a nation permanently great, consisting for greater part of wretched and miserable families."

Moreover, the effect upon ourselves of consenting to, or assisting in causing the debasement—physical, intellectual or moral—of our fellow-creatures, must react upon and lower our own moral qualities.

Anyone, therefore, will probably easily admit that if it be possible this justice should enter into our relations with our fellow-beings in business life. The very numerous laws contained in the statute books of this State, especially in the sanitary code, show that in fact we do recognize this principle in isolated cases. It is part of the police power of the State, which, as defined by our Court of Appeals (98 New York, 98), "is very broad and comprehensive, and is exercised to promote the health, comfort, safety and welfare of society."

As to the theoretical desirability of the admission of these higher principles of justice into business life, there can probably be little doubt; the only question is how that can be rendered possible in the present state of society?

In my opinion, our views of what is just already play a much larger part in business life than is generally acknowledged by writers on political economy. Are not the wages of the most unskilled laboring men fixed by the amount of physical comforts which their employers think it necessary to allow them, over and above the means necessary for the bare support of life? And from these wages required to realize the lowest ideals of life, do not wages grade upwards in various stages as the skill or strength required in the work increases? So that finally the rate of wages is determined by the ideas of justice in regard to compensation for the rudest forms of labor among the employers; and we have seen what an influence the most selfish of a class of employers have in reducing wages.

Sir John Lubbock says in the above cited article on the early closing movement: "It seems clear that nothing but legislation can remedy the evil. Voluntary action has been tried and failed over and over again, and the almost unanimous opinion of the witnesses examined before the House of Commons committee was that it was hopeless to expect any shortening of the hours in that way. Such, then, is the present position of affairs, and, as I have said, the general feeling of the shopkeeping community is in favor of legislation. Even as long ago as 1873 the shopkeepers who came to me with reference to the bill I then proposed expressed themselves in favor of a general compulsory closing, I then thought this was impossible. Only by degrees have I become convinced how deep and general this feeling is."

The State can certainly regulate many evils if it will. It does regulate them to a certain extent; if the programme of Professor Sumner as to factory laws, hours of labor, etc., were carried out, we would probably be going as far as the circumstances at present require. The chief thing necessary at this time appears to me to be to recognize that these so-called interferences with the liberty of contract are justified in theory, and are not merely to be considered by the richer classes as victories wrung from them by ignorant masses acting against their own interests. All classes should take a lively interest in the adjustment of these questions, in the belief that their correct solution will afford a great and permanent good to all.

We should recognize once for all the general principle that no manufacture shall be carried on which, as a rule, produces sickness or prematurely shortens the lives of the individuals employed therein; that no dwellings or workshops shall exist which do not possess the sanitary conditions necessary to preserve the ordinary health of the inmates. The effect of carrying this principle into practice would be of course to stop every kind of business in which the employer could not or would not furnish the employees salubrious working-rooms and pay them sufficient to support themselves in a healthy and decent manner, in return for only so many hours of labor as would not overtax their strength, but allow them a fair, physical, mental and moral development.

According to the Massachusetts statistics of Labor Report of 1880: "The advancement of the workingman in an economic way, along with the best intellectual and moral training, is the only sure method to improve his social education, opportunities and life" (p. 244).

As John Stuart Mill said: "Education is not compatible with extreme poverty. It is impossible effectually to teach an indigent population" (p. 202 of "Political Economy").

Before proceeding, however, to enumerate the blessings which we all will acknowledge might flow from such an improvement in the condition of workingmen, let us examine the great objections which of course suggest themselves to any one. The first is, that such an extension of the sanitary laws, tenement-house inspection, etc., means the stopping of many business establishments which can earn only sufficient profits to pay their employees their present low wages. The natural consequence would be that these employees would be thrown out of work, and that the supply of the articles which they manufactured would decrease and the price thereof increase.

Depriving these people of their wages would doubtless be an evil, but is it a greater evil than allowing them to work on at their present occupations, ruin their health and become a burden on society? If there is not work enough for them in this locality, at wages which secure them a decent living, there is work in other places; or even if emigration were impossible, it is very certain that it would be a cheap price for society to pay to support even a large number of individuals of this generation at work on public undertakings, rather than to allow them to become each the fountain head of new misery and crime, which always springs from degraded humanity. The first English factory act was passed after an epidemic had started from the overcrowding of children in factories.

Of course, the enforcement of these sanitary laws would prevent the subsequent establishment of such poorly paying kinds of business, so that the burden above referred to would at most have to be borne only once for all. The saying is well known, "Abject poverty is the mother of crime." There is a sum in dollars and cents, and, if wages are below that, men are driven to crime and women to shame. Crime is increasing at an alarming ratio. According to Mr. Round, Secretary of the Prison Association of New York, in this city in 1850 the proportion of criminals to the number of inhabitants was 1 in 3,000; in 1870, it was 1 in 1,021; in 1881, it was 1 in 837. According to the same authority, $480,000,000 are annually paid to protect society from criminals. This item of the expense to society to protect itself against its internal foes is increasing too rapidly to be borne. As a business matter, in order to save money, working men and women must be put in better circumstances. The same can be said of intemperance, the root of which lies in overwork and underpay; alcohol is the cheapest food for giving temporary strength.

Next, let us consider the objection that the stopping of these factories would raise the price of the commodities which they heretofore produced. These commodities would be either articles of luxury or of necessity. If they were articles of luxury, the loss would fall upon the rich, and, in my opinion, anyone who contemplates the increase in luxury, during the last fifty years, will conclude that a certain decrease in that direction can well be borne. If, however, the manufactures were articles of necessity it is true that their price would rise, and that this would bear hard particularly on the poor. But, if the price of living of all workingmen were raised, while the sanitary and other laws continued to be enforced, the wages of workingmen would have to be raised in proportion. So that the loss would again fall upon the wealthy classes, and would lead them to diminish their expenditures for luxury, which, as above observed, they can, in my opinion, well afford to do, and, perhaps, most of all, to their own profit. Moreover, self-interest directs the community, merely for the sake of decreasing the price of an article to a class of consumers, not to allow employers to reduce the wages of their employees, or to force them to work under such unfavorable circumstances as to unfit them for profitable labor at an early age, and thus compel society to support them and their families.

Of the advantages which would compensate all classes for this sacrifice in artificial luxuries, it is needles to speak in detail; in the words of Ruskin, we would have instead of " cities in which the object of man is not life but labor; cities in which the streets are not the avenues for the passing processions of a happy people, but the drains for the discharge of a tormented mob," cities " whose walls shall be safety, and whose gates shall be praise."

Finally, however, it will occur to many, that we have in late years in this country and abroad passed many laws for the inspection of tenement houses, factories, etc., and yet there has been no corresponding improvement in the condition of the workingmen, if there has been any ; that many of these laws remain dead letters or are used by corrupt officials as the means of private emolument ; and that consequently we have little reason to suppose that the mere extension of this principle will produce any real benefit to the workingmen or to society at large. In answer to this argument, I would refer to my former paper on "Trade Organizations in Public Affairs or Federalism in Cities," in which I have endeavored to show that the great cause of the mal-administration of our municipal affairs is our adherence to the antiquated and false system of electing our city fathers, legislators and judges of inferior courts from artificial geographical districts, in which the gin-shop influence is certain to be paramount, instead of from the city at large, where the men of all classes might select those who are to make and to enforce their laws according to their untrammeled wishes. So long as this system of artificial divisions of cities remains, with its corrupt ramifications, so long will any extension of the powers of government, even in the interest of humanity and justice, be failures. Consider for a moment the character of the man who now occupies the position of head of our Board of Health; would not those laws be differently enforced if the organizations of employees, for whose protection they are intended, had some direct influence in selecting this official? Governor Seymour well defined self-government (as cited in my paper above referred to) as attempting "to distribute each particular power to those who have the greatest interest in its wise and faithful exercise." Any excessive demands of the workingmen would certainly be met if these demands were publicly discussed by the arguments of the representatives of the employers and of all other interests in the city or State, and would yield before the moral weight of this united opinion; especially as the various classes of workingmen learned that they themselves were consumers as well as producers; and that an increase in the wages of one class meant an increase in the price of the article which that class produced.

No matter how far this principle of justice were carried into economical matters, it would never produce equality of property. The past is not to be obliterated; different types of men possess different degrees of force and intelligence; the rise and fall of individuals and races must continue; but we can at least by this plan do much to secure to all within our city and State and ultimately within our nation, a much happier and safer life than they lead at present, and as I believe, one that will make all our citizens once more contented and patriotic. Human hands may never build Jerusalem the Golden, but we can give all our fellow-citizens opportunity to live a healthy, moral life here and to prepare themselves for a life in the world to come.

www.ingramcontent.com/pod-product-compliance
Lightning Source LLC
Chambersburg PA
CBHW022015220426
43663CB00007B/1085